MW01610988

Father Knows Best

Letting Go, Looking Upward, and Leaning on the Lord

By Deborah R. Houston

Printed in the United States of America

First Printing: April 2010

ISBN-978-0-615-36926-6

TABLE OF CONTENTS

*This book is dedicated to — first and foremost — my
Heavenly Father. You have always known me, kept me,
and continue to hold me in the palm of Your hand.
You are worthy of all praise and honor. You are to be
glorified and exalted above all.*

*To my husband, for his gift of love and support
and the reminder that God is good all of the time
and all of the time, God is good.*

*To my daughters, for the joy only they can bring. It is
an honor and a privilege to be your mother.*

*To my mentor, for the cool in you, your constant prayers
and encouragement, the example of strength and a life
that exhibits the peace only He can give.*

To my parents, my siblings and my family.

*To all who have encouraged me, known me, prayed for
and with me, and even those that I have yet to meet, for
our soon-to-be encounter is a blessing from God.*

☫
PRAISE FOR DEBORAH R. HOUSTON'S
FATHER KNOWS BEST

Father Knows Best is a thrilling, page-turning autobiography. It is a ten-chapter journey into the life of a woman who shares not only her spiritual journey, but also the challenges of an African-American woman growing up in a family dealing with the daily struggles of life in the ghetto.

It speaks of a daughter's love for a man who is a contradiction. At times he is a loving father and husband; on the other hand, he is a crack-dealing lowlife who is loved unconditionally by his daughter and feared by others.

The book also deals with a strained relationship between a mother and a daughter both looking for acceptance and love from the same man.

This real-life drama is written in a captivating style that will make you not want to put it down. It will force you to look at your own life and the relationships you have with your parents, your siblings, and your God. It speaks about the vicissitudes of life that we all face and the decisions we make, as well as the consequences of those decisions—good or bad. This true story will make you think about the impact environmental and social surroundings have on our development as human beings.

Father Knows Best is real and exhilarating; it will make you cry, laugh, and say amen. I am so proud of my wife, the mother of my children, my friend and my sister in Christ.

With all of my love,
Dr. Jerry G. Houston (author's husband)

For years I've listened as you talked about growing up in the inner city and the countless lessons learned throughout those years. I've listened as you've talked about how those lessons impacted your life, how they shaped your thought processes and molded your decision making. However, none were more poignant than the lessons you learned from your father.

As you shared your experiences growing up, I witnessed your personal journey of developing a relationship with Christ and how you— allowed the Heavenly Father to transform your life into a life of purpose.

Now you're able to share real-life examples from your experiences in such an engaging way that it makes this book a "must read," and your readers will want to read it again, and again, and again!

This book not only chronicles the life of a child raised in the shadow of her father's emotional baggage, but also provides practical advice for anyone seeking emotional control once God's will is manifested in their spirit.

True spiritual growth requires prayer, and I can think of no better way to support a friend than by lifting them up in prayer on a daily basis. I have been privileged to watch your spiritual growth and to witness you surrender yourself completely to God.

I've watched you transform from a self-controlled, self-reliant, strong-willed young woman to a gracious, outgoing, radiant, mature woman with a gift that God now uses to inspire women from all walks of life. Accordingly, you've been able to effectively transfer your spiritual journey to the pages of this writing. Now you have trusted Him who is able to do exceedingly, abundantly above all that we can ask or think— and it is finished.

> With the love of a friend,
> Jacqueline Dulin (author's mentor)

PREFACE

I am every woman. I am an inquisitive child raised in the hood, aware of her surroundings, absorbing everything and asking enough questions to make heads spin. I am the teenager who struggles to understand a society that refuses to listen, full of zeal to step out into the unknown and capture what rightfully belongs to me—though my actions are seen as rebellion.

I am the student yearning to learn, yet lacking the wisdom to effectively apply the knowledge received, vowing to never give up. I stand as the young woman who desperately searches for her identity, realizing that the world can be her stage.

I am the wife who strives to make a comfortable home for her family by meeting the needs of her husband, often going without for the sake of others, while caring for children and wearing the hats of chef, accountant, judge, chauffeur, doctor, seamstress, etc., knowing that time waits for no one, and with each day, strength is renewed.

I am the friend that is loyal to her sisters, prays for them, keeps their secrets, doesn't always agree, but respects and embraces their totality.

I am the mother who watches her children grow, eagerly anticipates their triumphs and challenges, and remains on her knees for them, with forever-open arms and unconditional love.

I am the divorced woman who searches for peace within,

often misunderstood, wrongfully judged and convicted for searching for and grabbing hold of the life that she deserves.

I sit as a grandmother rocking in her chair, looking over her life, longing to pass on the wisdom that's housed in her gray hairs. Her hands, soft, yet worn, speak of years gone by, while the etched lines of age and weariness could never compare to the strength of her heart that beats in the hopes of her grandchildren touching this world in a positive manner.

I am every woman. In the words of the 1972 feminist anthem, "I am woman, hear me roar." My roar has been silenced for too long; however, the blame lies with me. I allowed my pain, my shame, my insecurities, and the ignorance of who I am destined to be, to hush my sound, changing it to a whisper and then ultimately resulting in its absence. My words bounced around in my brain, as opposed to being freed to be heard, and it was my fault. I quenched my own spirit. I placed my voice on lockdown—not in the literal sense, for I could speak, but I wasn't being true to myself; therefore, I silenced the woman within.

But today, my voice comes forth as a roar and declaration of God's goodness, His mercy, His love, His peace, and His joy. All of which exist when we, as His children, trust in His promises, lean on His everlasting arms, abide in His sovereignty, and live with the assuredness that...Father Knows Best.

PROLOGUE

It has been said that within the family unit, relationships are born and bonds are established that, in many cases, are unbreakable. For the bond is so strong, so thick, so heavy and filled with loyalty—an unconditional loyalty—that very rarely can it be broken. One bond formed, I believe, starts in the womb of a mother carrying her unborn child. There's a nurturing characteristic that has been instilled in every woman, especially mothers. It's a nurturing that begins as life grows inside of her womb, sometimes unknown to her; the motherly instinct brings with it an unconditional love, a die-hard sense of protection and an eternal bond.

Something can be said about this bond, for when a woman carries a man-child, it's the son who lovingly feels the need to protect and look after his mother. It's the son who longs to please his mother. It's the mother's eyes that light up when looking upon the face of her son, and it's a mother's heart that is intertwined within the beat of her son's heart.

Perhaps it's because we, as humans, are meant to bond with those who are opposite of ourselves. Qualities we don't possess are found in the other. That person—our opposite— holds what we do not.

It could be that while the mother carries this male child, the unmistakable difference in DNA causes a bond to form that lasts a lifetime. But, it seems that sons steal their mother's heart, pull at her heartstrings, wrap their fingers around her soul, and a bond is created that is one of love—undying and unconditional.

I have yet to truly understand this bond, for I am not the mother of yet-to-be men. However, the same can be said for another bond that exists within the family unit, that of father and daughter. This bond begins when the father first sees his female child. His heart becomes full and the masculine, mannish, hard-core persona melts within; he immediately takes on the role of protector, teacher, and sometimes savior.

This is the father's "baby girl," even when the child becomes a mother of her own and long into her adult years. She brings out his softer side. She brings out his smile. She takes his rough exterior, apparent in his sometimes calloused hands (depending on his occupation), and has the ability to turn a man that could be seen as a powder keg waiting to explode into baby powder.

Even though they weren't known unto each other until birth, it is love at first sight. I have seen this look in a father's eyes. I have witnessed the melting of the heart for I was a "daddy's girl." The oldest and first daughter of a man, which means that I captured his heart upon my birth. Being the pure, clean, unsoiled, new-to-sin newborn, I erased all of his dirt, his shady dealings, or anything that he'd ever done wrong. If he never did anything else right again, I was the one thing that was right in his world—his baby girl.

Upon my birth, we shared a bond, like most fathers and daughters; however, being an infant, I did not know of its existence. As an infant, I was oblivious to it, but even then, his deep voice could calm me when I cried or cause me to squeal with laughter. He was my father, a man who lived in a world that didn't understand where he'd come from, didn't care that he existed, and didn't want to know where he was going, for not only was he a man—he was a black man. However, because he aware of his color, though he attempted to make it according to society's rules and regulations—some civilized and others not—he decided to make his own rules.

It tired him to live in a society that only held out its hand to give him leftovers. He became frustrated with the world only noticing him to make sure he wasn't getting too big for his britches, he wasn't too smart for his own good, he wasn't making too much money, or he stayed in his place. His place—a place that society created, so it could dictate the rules and boundaries.

My father seethed, his anger boiling. It exhausted his soul to watch the world when it slapped him into the place where it felt he belonged or strung up, locked up, or cut down those who dared to cross that invisible line.

And so, he created his own creed, beat his own drum, and kept his own rhythm. He decided to spit in their faces. He took it as long as he could, and then he made up his mind to do things his way.

His way was that of a street pharmacist, a drug dealer, slingin' the rock, the keeper of crack, and the list goes on and on.

He, being a boy from the country, never really understanding the ways of the city, learned quickly and worked hard. But, after years of trying to do it the honorable way, he took it upon himself, without seeking the advice of his wife, to start out small, sell a little "somethin'-somethin'," here and there. Business boomed, and he soon became "The Man" to see for whatever anyone needed—day or night.

Finally, after society refused to see him as a man, he took it upon himself to create his own space, his own title, and generate respect from those who were overlooked, for they too were numbered with those considered to be less than men.

He was more reliable than the postman, regardless of the sleet, snow, rain, or shine. He was always available to get or give what was wanted, as long as the money came back strong.

My father did this for years and he became "that man." The man that people looked at differently now. Some gazed upon him with honor; others saw him as the neighborhood Robin

Hood, the savior of the west side. Others glared with jealousy as "benjamins" rolled in, but all stepped to him with respect. It was this newfound respect from others that caused him to look upon himself differently. It no longer mattered to him that what he had been taught once upon a time was right and wrong; those things were now defined by the future that he wanted, and the respect that he needed to be seen as a man—by any means necessary.

Things didn't go down in the neighborhood unless he knew about it; if a wrong had been done, it was handled with street justice and when he walked with his steel-toe boots, taking long strides down the block, people stepped aside. Other men, wanting and hoping to be seen as men, acknowledged him with a nod of their heads in a reverential kind of way.

Women of all shapes and sizes who never noticed him before or even thought of giving him the time of day—no matter how strong his rap was—now either swooned for his power or smirked because he had been with them recently or tossed them aside after being with them.

He was the Robin Hood of the ghetto. The CEO of a dynasty that operated better than any Fortune 500 company because with all that he did, not once was he arrested. Do I find pride in what he did and the way that he did what he did? No. Lives were destroyed, families were torn apart, and he thrived off the weak. There's no glory in inflicting pain or havoc on those that need and long for help, even if they don't realize their need.

However, I recognize that in being raised by him, living with him, and learning from him, he taught me lessons that I shall never forget. Lessons that were embedded in my brain. Lessons that were taught and drilled into my skull to be cited and recited, practiced, and never forgotten.

Today, as a woman standing on my own without this "father", I find myself remembering his lessons. And as I journey towards who I am as a result of his lessons, I realize that the bond—though forever remaining—must be broken. I ask myself if that very thing is possible, for its strands are woven into my psyche, my memory, my life. However, if it is to be severed, cut, or perhaps take on a new meaning besides that of a bond, I am not the one to make that change. I may not have the strength to sever such ties.

It is here that I stand, as a woman, a new woman, a new creature, realizing that I also have another Father. This is the Father that must take my bond and my ties to the past, and create a new bond to be shared with Him. For it is Him from whom I've also learned lessons, for He knew me before anyone else. He knew me before my mother or father was aware of my existence, for He created me, and has made me His own, giving me the name of Daughter. And it's His lessons that have taught me to be better, to live better, to love better, and to do better. His lessons have transformed my spirit; they continue to mold my being and shape me into a woman that continues to learn from her past and can now look forward to her future, as I place an unwavering faith in Him, realizing that Father Knows Best.

LESSON ONE
Crying Is For the Weak

"Pow! Pow! Pow!" The sound rang in my ears on a hot summer day, as the car seemed to drift by in slow motion. My feet froze when I heard the dangerous sound. The sound forced men, women, boys, and girls to scramble for shelter, as the bullet casings bounced on the hot asphalt below. The continued succession of bullets being fired snapped me back into reality; the signal from my brain finally reached my feet, so that they could move and move quickly. These bullets were an alarm informing me that something was coming. They meant eminent danger, the vapor of hatred, the possibility of death, and the messenger of a life's lesson. The first lesson of many that would be embedded into my mind, bored into my soul, and carried in my spirit until it was exorcised, freeing me to live and love. This was a day like any other, but then again, it wasn't.

It's just another day in the hood. A hot and sunny day when kids run around playing neighborhood games. Boys slamming a basketball into a cutout milk crate nailed to a wooden telephone pole, using moves like they're on the court of the NBA. The rhythmic sound of wired rope smacking the pavement, while girls twirl it in their hands playing double-dutch. The whoosh of kids zooming up and down the cracked pavement on their Big Wheels or banana-seat bicycles with the handlebar tassels blowing in the wind. Hearts beating in time with the bass booming from the radio of a car driving by. Teenage girls walking up and down the pavement as if on a

Paris catwalk, hair in cornrows or Afro puffs, wearing tight and colorful halter tops to show off their budding womanhood while miniskirts hug their thighs, making the "brothas" gathering at the corner suspend their dice game for a chance to whoop and holler for attention, as their mouths water at the fantasy of untouched youthfulness.

It's summertime. Nobody's thinking about time or being inside of a hot row house. Even the women sit out on the stoop, popping gum, sipping on Pepsi-Colas and wiping their kids' sticky lips and fingers from the sugary sweet water ice, while some men congregate on another stoop smoking cigarettes.

It's summertime. The stifling heat is intensified by the lack of space due to a city crowded with high-rise buildings and row homes that limit the ability for a breeze to blow freely, but that doesn't stop people from filling the streets. Some choose to remain inside, sitting in front of a box window fan that does nothing more than circulate hot air, but a hot breeze is better than none at all.

It's summertime. The buses, cars, trolleys, and subways expel their clouded exhaust into the air, adding to the sweltering heat that blankets the city with a layer of smog that city dwellers breathe in and out on a daily basis— the original secondhand smoke.

The sun bakes the asphalt and turns the pavement into a sizzling stone, but the winos, lying on the trash-strewn sidewalk, still clutch their bottles with the fierceness of a baby's lips wrapped around a pacifier. To take the bottles away would evoke an immediate cry.

Mutts and cats roam the alleys barking, meowing, and looking for a handout, while passers-by don't give them a second look. It's summertime.

I never gave any thought to our having money or not having money, or being considered living below or above the poverty line. I didn't know such things existed. I was oblivious to whether our home was confined in the midst of boundaries known as the ghetto. It was what it was.

As with all summer days in the hood, I never thought this day would be any different than any other hot summer day. My friends and I did the same old things we did on every summer day, whether that included participating in some imaginary game, making new rules for an old game, or simply sitting on the stoop and taking a break from all of the games. Nothing seemed out of the ordinary.

The smells were still the same. A mixture of damp, sticky heat baking the black-tarred streets, fried chicken sizzling in the row houses, the stench of urine that watered the weeds in the alley, cheap liquor fermenting in bottles thrown in the gutters, and our own sweat. It was just another day.

The sounds were the same. Kids' fast footsteps, men cussing loudly, dogs barking, the monotonous music of the ice cream truck that was blocks away—causing kids to dig deep into their pockets hoping to find change instead of lint, and the booming bass from the car radios that passersby could feel in their chests—causing hearts to beat in time with the rhythm. It appeared to be an ordinary day in the hood.

Car wheels screeched around the corner giving everyone a hint of its high speed.

I saw it coming. My friends and I were taking a break, sitting on my front steps. We had become tired of playing games and parked our bikes against the fence or the steps, or threw them haphazardly on the ground. As it approached, everything moved in slow motion. I heard the yells and screams, but couldn't decipher what was being said. One of the four young men in the car leaned out, shooting a gun, as the car moved. People darted in all different directions. Behind parked cars, under cars, in their front yards, into homes that weren't even theirs, wherever and whatever it took to get away. My friends scattered, and I never even saw them leave. My feet were frozen. My entire body seemed to comply with my feet, except for my eyes. They darted back and forth, absorbing everything around me, until they became fixed on the car, the boys inside, and the gun that was being fired.

I saw the driver, and our eyes locked on each other. He looked at me, and all of the sounds around me ceased. The driver was a young man that I knew. If a person lived in the ghetto long enough, he or she knew everybody, had heard of them, or knew someone that they knew. As the seconds passed, our eyes continued to focus on each other. His face didn't hold a smile, a grimace, or a frown; he almost appeared to look through me. In reality, our eyes locked for a split second, but it seemed like an eternity. It was almost as if our eyes were trying to pass on a coded message to one another, but before I could decipher the code, our gaze into each other's world was halted by the yank on my arm.

The pull that I felt didn't seem real. It was strong, but for some reason, I resisted. At first, I didn't know who was pulling me or why, but I soon realized that the hand that had wrapped itself around my wrist was trying to pull me into my home. Still, I resisted. It was as if the driver or the events unfolding had a hypnotic hold on my body, and I wasn't ready to go inside. I understood the extent of the danger. I knew that the bullets, the gun, and the boys in the car were real, but I refused to go inside without—of all things—my bike, my beloved purple bike with the white banana seat, the white basket hooked on the handle bars, and the neon sparkling streamers that whipped in the wind when I flew up and down the street.

During children's toddler years, they become territorial and protective of whatever they feel rightfully belongs to them. Their cries of independence are just one word, "Mine!" I imagine my toddler's brain engaged, wanting to protect something that belonged solely to me.

How could I leave my bike out there alone to be shot up? I didn't want to go, but the pull was greater than my resistance, as my body was lifted into our home, and I never felt my feet touch any of the four steps leading into our enclosed porch.

I hollered, I screamed, I reached for my bike, but to no avail; the door was slammed shut behind me. I was separated from it.

"Smack!" The sound reverberated on our enclosed porch as the hand left my face stinging and red, silencing my cries.

"Shut up!" My vocal chords obeyed the command, either out of shock from the unexpected slap or the fear of receiving another one, as tears seemed to freeze in midstream down my face. I looked up into dark eyes.

I should've known how stupid it was to fear losing the life of something that doesn't have any life. It was just a bike. None of my other friends had given their bikes a second thought. They were left abandoned in front of our home, along with my own.

My mother, the slap deliverer, dropped her open hand to her side. I ran to my father for comfort and confirmation of the necessity of my tears, but his eyes betrayed me before his voice spoke. Today, he was not going to be my savior. He was not going to chastise his wife for executing the discipline he had always previously condemned. Instead, his massive rough hands encircled my arms to make sure I would never forget his words, "Crying is for punks, the weak! If I ever see you cry, I'll give you a reason to cry!" The well of tears yet-to-be-spilled dried up inside my soul and on that day—a day that started out like any other—I realized that I was not supposed to cry. I was not allowed to cry. I don't even know if I had been told before, but today was the day I learned the lesson that tears were forbidden.

Her slap and his words taught and confirmed that tears were a sign of weakness only to be shed by those who couldn't handle the task or the situation. It meant that the only reward for shed tears would be punishment as opposed to sympathy, empathy, or comfort. It defined for me that even if tears needed to be shed or released, it was prohibited; therefore, they must be shed within—unknown to anyone else. It was a day unlike any other day, but then again, it wasn't.

How does one cry when they've always been taught that crying is basically a sin? How can tears be shed and the well within one's soul released after it has been on lockdown for years and decades? I could outwardly laugh, be angry, have remorse, compassion, and all other emotions, but this emotion where tears needed to spill over and be shown was condemned. I was allowed to experience various emotions, but tears were to be hidden and kept within the soul—where no one would see them.

The lesson of the prohibition of tears was often repeated in my childhood home, and I wondered about its origin. I wondered what made my father's heart so hard that it could not be pricked to release tears. What made the foundation of his heart ground so dry that it was probably cracked, because it had not been watered by his tears?

As a child, I never contemplated these things. I simply obeyed and did as I was told, thinking this was the way it had to be. It was best, and those who passed this lesson on knew better than I did. However, as an adult, I longed to know of the original teacher who supplied this lesson to my father. I wanted to know who passed this lesson on to him or whether something had happened to teach him this lesson.

It wasn't until my adult years that I was confronted with what I had been taught and practiced. When I was blessed with children of my own, I realized that the lesson that started with my father, and was passed on to me, was being handed down to my own children.

I don't know how many times I had encouraged my children not to cry, to suck it up, or to run away from the desire to cry. It didn't dawn on me until one day, my child cried, and I reprimanded her for doing so. At that moment, it was as if I was catapulted back in time to our enclosed porch, as I heard my father speaking through me, and I shook with fear. Instead of passing on the slap that I received, I covered my mouth with my own hand, hoping to stifle the thought that had already escaped my brain and slowed through my lips. Instead of delivering a slap, I held my child close and allowed her to cry. I allowed her to shed tears that I was never allowed to shed, and I vowed to never repeat the lesson to my children or anyone else. I don't even recall her reason for crying, but by doing so, she shed them for me as well—until I was able to cry myself. And it would take years for me to do so. Her allowance was not my own. I allowed my child to cry, and my reasons could have been because she was simply a child, yet I was an adult. The lesson had been given to me, and it was my job to honor it, not hers. Still, I had to take baby steps. I wasn't ready for the confrontation of the power of tears. I had to be reprogrammed, watch, and learn from others whom I respected that it was okay to cry.

It wasn't until some years later that I was first confronted with the power of tears, while sitting in a restaurant with my mentor who was dealing with the illness of her older sister. I listened as she spoke of her concern, her worries, and her doubts. Her words told of her frustration with the inability to ease the pain of her loved one and to even control the pain. As my mentor, her words always spoke volumes to me, but while she spoke, it was that one single and lonely tear silently inching down the left side of her face that became magnified in my vision and my mind.

To say that I found myself at a loss for words is an understatement. Here was a woman who I had a great amount of respect for, and she allowed her soul to flood. Of course, I had seen many others shed tears, but the lesson taught to me, and that I embraced, told me that these people were weak—

they didn't know how to keep it all together. They weren't in control of their emotions, and they didn't know any better. I even felt sorry for them, and told myself they didn't have the luxury of the lesson that I had been given. Yet, here in front of me, in a public place, my mentor—whom I adored—shed a tear that spoke volumes to my soul.

This was my mentor, the woman that had taken me under her wing to teach me her perspective of life, who shared with me the goodness of God and who I admired for her remarkable faith, wisdom, and strength. I watched helplessly as this woman sat in front of me doing what I had been taught not to do. To cry. To allow the well to overflow—not within but without. This woman sat before me without fear of being ridiculed for shedding a tear. I considered her to be strong, and now as I watched this tear escape and find its way down her face, my definition of strength was being challenged.

This was the moment in my life when all of the lessons taught to me were shattered and put into question. I had to ask myself, is it possible that what I've been taught has been wrong? This moment was the beginning of my self-examination and self-discovery, becoming the woman that God had already destined for me. I had to reevaluate everything within and move toward a new direction for myself and my children.

It was this lesson, one of many unspoken lessons taught by my mentor, that caused me to realize the powerful God we serve. The God whose servant David informs and reminds us in Psalm 139:14 that "we are fearfully and wonderfully made" inside and out. Our outward appearance—length or quality of Clairol-colored or uncolored hair; shade or texture of skin, whether baby-soft or wrinkled and worn; and even height, width, and size—is not what makes us fearfully and wonderfully made. It is the woman within, the character deep within our souls that speaks of who we truly are. It is true that the external—our style, as well as our fashion sense—exemplifies a reflection of the internal. But, first and foremost, upon His creation of us, we were molded, shaped, and formed as being fearfully and wonderfully made. And that includes our hearts, our minds, and yes, even our tears.

Each part of our anatomy was designed for a purpose, as an expression of edification of one another and glorification of the fear-conquering God we serve and the wonder-working power He possesses and instills in each and every one of us. And yes, this anatomy even includes our tear ducts.

The magnification of my mentor's tear was branded into my mind, urging me to investigate and to understand its origin and its meaning. That one, single tear spoke to my soul, challenged my beliefs, and watered my hardened exterior.

It was during my investigation that I learned of the purpose of a tear—how even our tears attest to His power in creating us to be fearfully and wonderfully made. From a scientific standpoint, mammals can shed tears when they are in pain; however, it is only humans who can shed tears because of emotions. Tears were given to us as an expression of the emotions felt within our spirits. Emotions of joy at the witness of love during a wedding ceremony, birth of a child, graduation of a student, or just receiving good news. We shed tears as a result of sadness due to an incredible loss— the passing of a loved one, the pain of a lost friendship, or the even the loss of employment. Tears are released for fear of the unknown; they can be shed due to relief, and we even shed tears of anger.

However, I had the most amazing revelation after discovering my Savior shed tears at the grave of His dear friend Lazarus in John 11:35. If my Lord was able to shed tears, why couldn't I do the same? He gave them to me—not as a sign of weakness or shame, but strength.

Contrary to what I'd been taught, it takes more strength to release a tear than to suppress it. Although I have never told my mentor these exact words, her solitary tear seeped into my heart, watered my soul, and unlocked a well of tears that had never been shed. I continue to come into the full reality that I am fearfully and wonderfully made, realizing He gave tears to me for a reason as an emotional being. I had to investigate whether there are other reasons for this gift of tears. What other lesson did my Father have for me in the form of tears?

I learned that tears lubricate our eyes. They keep our eyes from being dry, which enables us to be able to blink. However—even more important— when we allow ourselves to cry, it's our tears that clean the surface of our eyes, washing away those microscopic things that the naked eye could never see, helping us to be able to see more clearly. "The eyes are the window to the soul" is an old proverb. If true, how magnificent it is that God would bless us with tears to be shed in order to clear our vision; therefore, freeing our souls to be better instruments used for His glory.

I've heard many women share with me how "sometimes you just need a good cry." According to them, once those tears have fallen, the pressure or weight is lifted—not that the circumstances have miraculously disappeared, but the built-up, emotional stress bursts forth like a dam that can no longer hold the swelling currents of water.

In reading Psalm 139:14 and understanding King David's words, I had to redirect my focus not only on being fearfully and wonderfully made, but also I had to embrace the first four words of this verse—"I will praise thee." I will praise God, and the reason for my praise is because I am fearfully and wonderfully made. I will praise Him for my tear ducts, for they enable me to release the tears that need and longed to be shed. As I grow in Him and accept His divine will and love for me, I will even praise Him for the circumstances for which the tears are shed. Because, even in the darkest of moments or the deepest pain, my Father continues to cradle me in His arms and assures me that He will never leave me nor forsake me. I will praise Him because in creating me, He knew of the purpose that was instilled in me to touch this world for Him. I will praise Him for keeping me when I never had an inkling that I needed keeping. I will praise Him for His goodness, His mercy, His shelter, and His provisions. I will praise Him for the journey of my life, the ups and the downs, the hurdles and the potholes, and even the trials and tribulations. I will praise Him, because in those moments when my strength seemed to wane, it was only because of Him that I could take another step and move forward. I will even praise Him for the moments when I had to be still and allow Him to lead me, guide me, direct me, and protect me. I will praise Him for loving me in spite of my faults, and—most of all—I will praise Him for being my God.

Now, the shackles from the well within my soul have been unlocked, and when and if tears are shed, it is because they were given to me by my Father. Not for show, display, or attention, but they attest that I am a human being, a woman of God, destined to be used for His glory. One who was and continues to be fearfully and wonderfully made, as I am purged with each tear to embrace the victory in knowing that "weeping may endure for a night, but joy comes in the morning" (Psalm 30:5).

LESSON TWO

Watch Your Own Back

Public school students in our city witnessed a fight at least every other day. Kids would gather around in wide-eyed anticipation, watching the warriors square off at each other for something as simple as "I heard that you said that I..." Sometimes the participants did not bother to clarify whether or not the supposed rumor was true. The fact that something could have been said challenged pride and reputation in the hood, which demanded immediate action. The crowd would usually be filled with friends of the combatants and/or relatives ready to jump in if their friend, "homie," or family member couldn't seem to handle his own business, which then resulted in it being everybody's business.

All of the fights during my childhood usually escalated to gang status quickly. Those considered strong, in an effort to remain so, always threatened the weak. Most of the fights involved kids that attended the public school system.

So, parents in my neighborhood who wanted a decent education for their kids would enroll them in private school—if they could afford it. Most of the time, their choice was a Catholic school where nuns, draped in starched, black cloaks with faces encircled in white wimples, had a reputation for being strict and dispensing discipline whenever necessary.

A few of my friends walked to the closest Catholic school wearing crisp, starched, blue, yellow, and green plaid uniforms with the required yellow shirts, blue knee socks and blue shoes. Never professing to be Catholic, they wore these ensembles every day; it was just part of the dress code for the students.

Luckily, my parents didn't send me to Catholic school. I didn't want to have to wear the same outfit every day. Those nuns never smiled. Their faces always seemed pasty white, as if they didn't know that the sun existed. Their narrowed eyes and thin-as-a-pencil lips told me they didn't like kids. Who knows what they carried under those long, black dresses? I didn't fear them; I just didn't appreciate the look of them.

In order to salvage my young and impressionable mind, keep me safe, and offer me a better education, my parents enrolled me in a private school an hour outside of the city where people that looked and lived like me—black folk— were scarce. In fact, I was the only black girl in my class for quite some time. As the years went by; however, there were a handful of black students, but we were still the definite minority.

Because my school was so far away, by the time I arrived home during the fall and winter months, it was almost dark. I wasn't able to hang out with my friends, for we were all hibernating in our ghetto homes.

People in the hood admired the snow, but rarely felt the need to venture out into it, unless necessary. Cold temperatures were usually less admired. We preferred to entertain ourselves within, rather than venture outward. But, as spring rolled around and the darkness began to lift a little earlier, giving way to later sunsets, children and adults longed for the sun's warmth and began to come out of hiding.

We would chat about our schools, our teachers, and our grades. But mostly, we talked about anxiously looking forward to getting away from it all. My friends and I would venture from the front of one house to another, shooting the breeze, laughing, and enjoying one another's company, without even realizing that we had formed our own little gang. It was not a gang that dispensed violence, but silently spoke of a camaraderie among us that started during our infant stroller days, while moms pushed us along. This bond continued through our Big Wheel, bicycle, skateboard, and double-dutch jumping days. We were friends bound together by our block, our turf, and our street.

We never fought like the hard-core street gangs; we were too cute for that. We were too busy calling our little gang the black Charlie's Angels, or we'd choose another label that spoke of our fineness and sense of adventure. Sometimes, we even tried to dress alike, wearing the same color jeans or pants, T-shirts, sneakers, and hairstyles. We were friends, a gang all our own that didn't take too kindly to the other neighborhood girls—especially the ones that lived one street over.

Our beef with one another usually only went as far as the usual catty dialogue that can float from the lips of little girls, but if not properly placed in check, can escalate to women who are scorned. Phrases such as "You think you cute," "you ain't cute," "you one conceited little heifer," "don't use my name in vain," "ya'll stuck up," "who you looking at," "don't start nothing," and "won't be nothing" rarely developed into blows, but always ended with "your momma!"

The rival girls tried to rock their clothes in one accord like we did, but they never could compare to us. We knew it and they knew it. We didn't hang with them and they didn't hang with us. When we passed each other without the backup of our friends—if we spoke, we spoke; if we didn't we didn't.

I had a personal beef with one of them because she always seemed to flaunt her stuff in front of the guys from our street. Sticking her butt out, laughing loud at nothing, popping her gum real loud—whatever it took to get attention. Not that I particularly cared for any of the guys she went for, it just seemed that the things she did were so degrading. Plus, I heard that she had already spread her legs open to boys in the alley several times; so, in my mind, she was a slut. She had a lot of mouth, always threatened to fight, but never put up when it counted and basically got on my nerves.

But no matter how much her antics got on my nerves, she didn't deserve what happened to her or her older sister. The two sisters attended Catholic school, the younger being my age while her sister was one year ahead of us.

Our neighborhood had quite a few "latchkey" kids. They had been given a set of keys to their home, so that once school was over, they could let themselves in and take care of themselves and possibly their younger siblings. Their responsibilities could range from fixing dinner for their entire family to doing laundry to other various tasks, until the caretaker came home from work.

There were also quite a few single parent homes in the hood, and the single parent was usually a woman. Many of these women were doing the best that they could to make a home for themselves and their children. However, I often wondered what happened to the fathers of most of these kids. What happened to cause them to drop in when they felt like it, and then leave when it suited them, only to be seen six months to a year later or longer? I wondered even more why that single mother would let the deadbeat dad back in. It was obvious that these men only came around for a "hit it and quit it" because they'd be gone before the sheets could cool off. My father told me that we were lucky to have both parents in the home, but that's only true if both of them are able to function in the expected, normal capacity.

The home where the rival girls lived was a single parent home where the mother was the caretaker. Although I did not know the father personally, I would see him around from time to time. Still, regardless of whether these two sisters were latchkey kids, came from a single parent home, or were rivals with the girls in our neighborhood, they didn't deserve what happened to them on that day, a day when my father taught me one of what he considered to be his most important lessons.

Earlier that day, but not known until later, the single mother and one of her drug-addicted, male relatives got into an argument. I never learned what the argument was about. But as insignificant as it might have been, a desperate drug user can throw it out of proportion and into a category of great importance. After the argument, the single mother left her home, while her relative remained, seething in anger.

Who knows what went through his mind during this moment of rage? Somewhere in his thought process, he decided to unleash anger on the first person to cross his path—which happened to be the older sister as she arrived home from Catholic school. I would imagine she greeted him as always. He wasn't a stranger, so she probably never saw the danger of him being there—after all, they were related. When she entered her home, as she had every day after school, she never realized that he was going to rape her, beat her to death, and leave her partially nude body wrapped in an old carpet in the basement.

The younger sister arrived home unaware of the fate that had befallen her older sister. She too, probably entered her home as usual, after leaving the Catholic school, thinking it was just another day. She met death on the second floor of their home when he strangled her.

The father probably dropped by, as he usually did from time to time, but didn't make it beyond the enclosed porch because he was later found lying in a pool of blood that seeped from a gaping wound, an ice pick protruding from the back of his skull.

As the unsuspecting single mother returned home, she was met with the dreaded devastation of the grisly murders—and no male relative anywhere.

My friends and I had no idea what had happened, as

police sirens filled the air with blue and red lights bouncing off the row homes, because sirens were a common occurrence. It wasn't until I was summoned home, and my father told me what had happened that I learned of that unfortunate family's fate. Our neighborhood was in shock. Even on ghetto terms, this was a shocking crime.

My mind was filled with so many questions, that I didn't even know where to begin. I wanted to know what happened. Who would hurt those girls like that? They weren't my friends, but no one deserved anything like that. My father told me that I was asking the wrong questions. He always impressed upon me to think before I spoke, questioned, or made a move. He told me that what was done, was done; my inquiries weren't right. I rethought my questions. So, I asked, how could one man bring harm to three individuals? How did it happen on different levels of the house? How did they walk into the death trap? From fear my questions spilled out, one after the other. I wanted to protect myself from meeting such a fate.

When my questions were asked to his satisfaction, my father sat me down, looked at me with his dark, menacing eyes, and spoke without emotion on the events that had transpired, giving one answer to my many questions. He said, "Sometimes you can't depend on the other person to be your lookout. Wherever you go, whatever you do, you gotta watch your own back."

This was his reasoning as to why these individuals had lost their lives. I watched him break down his philosophy, as he taught me that wherever I went, I had to act as if I had eyes in the back of my head. He told me to make sure that no one was following me, check behind myself often, and never leave a room with my back turned. His words were like those of a military soldier trained in tactical combat, and I carried his words with me throughout my life.

The moments of that day and his words changed my entrances and exits, my walking and running, in addition to molding my mind to believe that I held the security of my safety and well-being.

When I walked down the street, I frequently looked over my shoulder. Once I started to drive, my eyes would often dart into my rear-view mirror. If jogging, I was sure to check the path that I'd just left with a simple turn of the head. Even while leaving any place of business, a simple glance over my shoulder was required. His lesson taught me not to trust anyone—not even my friends and my homies. I was conditioned to believe that if anything ever went down, they would be sure to leave me to fall or take the fall. His words held the belief that everyone is a suspect; they always want something. No one is genuine; everyone is out for themselves and what they can get from you.

When a child is taught that trust is nonexistent, a wall is built. It's an impenetrable wall that can only be breached with the permission of the builder. It is a transparent wall that cannot be seen with the visible eye, but it is there, and each brick has been strategically placed by its builder, offering false security and comfort.

Each brick is molded from experiences solidifying the original lesson of distrust, and the mortar gripping each brick is the fear instilled by the lesson presenter.

The danger of residing within the confines of the wall occurs when the builder's identity is secured by the erection and stability of the wall—even though its very foundation is unstable. However, the person who resides behind the wall isn't aware that their insecurity is based on instability.

From my father's lesson, I began to build my wall. I was fearful and dared not trust. I looked at people with the expectation that they were incapable of ever truly caring, and their motivation was ultimately to take care of themselves. No one was to be trusted.

I was building a wall that I thought would protect me from the pain of distrust, and the only thing that could tear it down was the love of an almighty God. A God who met me where I was, cowering and hiding behind my wall, afraid to trust, afraid to live, and afraid to exist without my wall. I became so wary of people that I didn't know what it meant to relax and be at ease. I was forever on the lookout, forever waiting for the ball to drop. I couldn't afford to be caught off-guard. I had to be ready.

Even when I heard of the love of God, I was skeptical. I heard my mother talk of God quite often, and she would even take us to church. But, from where I was sitting, these people were in the same situation I was or worse—living in the hood, going nowhere, doing nothing, and watching time tick away. I was hearing, but not listening.

When I was confronted with the truth and actually listened, I began my journey of slowly tearing down my wall. I heard the gospel of Jesus Christ—that He died, was buried, and arose from the dead. I believed what I heard, and I repented of my sin. I confessed that Christ was the Son of God, and I was baptized for the forgiveness of my sins. I was now a child of God, a new creature. But, I was still operating under the same procedures, still living with the same habits. I was still holding on to and living by the lessons taught to me by my father, instead of allowing my Father to re-teach, remold, and reshape me.

I had to be taught and learn anew. Plans were in place for the destruction of the wall. But, still I was afraid to live a life freely in Him and in accordance with His Word. I allowed the mortar of fear to permeate my entire being; it was pumping in my veins. However, as His child, I had to be willing to trust Him without fear. The wall had to come down. In becoming His child, the destruction of my wall meant that I had to learn to trust Him more than I trusted myself.

It was a difficult task, for I was taught that to trust the mortal is a sin that leads to destruction, which I could visibly see and touch. How could I even begin to trust the immortal? If I was taught only to rely on my meager instincts to watch my own back, how was I to give my care and security to One I could not see?

However, to trust in God is to have faith that He will do as He promised, to rely on His promise, and to stand strong and secure in His promise. By becoming His child, I was confronted with the reality that He alone is the only one who could make such a promise to be with me at all times—"even until the end of this world"(Matthew 28:20).

I had to be willing to believe that He has been with me, is with me right now, and will continue to be with me. He is not confined by time or space, distance or depth. Due to His omnipresence and omnipotence, no one can do a better job of effectively watching my back and being my security than He can—my Father.

I had to learn and am still learning to allow Him to tear my wall down, brick by brick, and replace it with Him as my rock in a weary land. I am learning to lean on Him as opposed to relying on myself.

However, there are moments in my life when I feel pain, and like a child running from a monster, I retreat behind my wall. Feverishly, I grab the mortar of fear and begin to rebuild an insecure wall, vowing to never come out again. As I cower behind my wall, He stands with open arms, reassuring me that He is there with me, ready to help me take the first step towards the purpose He has already destined. Not behind a wall, but standing in a world full of people that need Him— some who know they need Him and others who don't. Some have built walls just like me for various reasons and need the assurance that only the Father can bring in tearing them down, for they were built on fear and distrust. As His child, I must live according to Edward Mote's "Solid Rock" hymn:

My hope is built on nothing less,
Than Jesus blood and righteousness.
I dare not trust a sweeter frame,
But wholly lean on Jesus' name.
Refrain:
On Christ the solid rock I stand,
All other ground is sinking sand;
All other ground is sinking sand.

It's because of my Father that I must stand for Him as I am, as only I can be—a woman full of His power and strong enough to venture beyond my fears. For as His child, He has "not given me a spirit of fear, but one of love and power and a sound mind" (II Timothy 1:7). It is in knowing my Father that I continue to realize that I don't have to watch my own back, because He has my past, my present, and my future in the palm of His hands.

LESSON THREE
Blood Is Thicker Than Water

Sunday dinners were usually held at my grandmother's home. She was, without a doubt, the queen of our family. It wasn't that my mother couldn't cook, although my father was the better of the two, but I think we went over there for a couple of reasons. First, the "shout-'til-you-pass-out" church we attended was way on the other side of town and was closer to my grandmother's home. By the time church ended, more than half the day was gone. Second, it was, basically, a tradition.

My grandmother had a whole tribe of kids, which seemed common back then. It wasn't unusual for a family to consist of ten to twelve children. I don't know if the prevalence of large families was because the women who bore them never heard of birth control, didn't care about birth control, didn't know how to use birth control, or didn't believe in birth control, but every Sunday we would pile into my grandmother's home where enough food was prepared to feed her army.

My grandmother, I'll refer to her as Queen—for that's what she was—and my aunts were in the kitchen talking, cooking, and fussing. My uncles were either huddled around the television watching sports or talking junk to one another, while the children were always sent outside to play. It was important for Queen to keep her crowded home as tidy as possible.

For that reason, the children were rarely allowed into the dimly lit living room, unless she felt the need to tickle the ivories of her dilapidated piano and needed a complacent audience who didn't care that she always played the same bluesy tune. It never mattered what lyrics Queen sang—gospel, R&B, or country. They were always overpowered by the same melody, her one and lonely piano piece. No matter how long she played her piano, we would stand around watching her sway to the music instead of sitting on the plastic-covered furniture, probably because it was more of a chore to peel away from the stiff, synthetic surface than to stand and listen.

The children, a brood of cousins, would tolerate it as long as we could, slowly inching our way toward the doorway. Seeing our efforts to retreat, Queen would finally dismiss us with a wave of her hand. It didn't matter though because we would rather be outside doing our own thing. But, we were careful not to venture too far. After all, this was the other side of town; it was not my turf and the rules were different.

Queen's hood was filled with Puerto Ricans with quick tempers and my own color folk who seemed to have run out of patience to deal with their own kind. It even looked like a war zone. There were more abandoned buildings than those that were actually occupied. The average city block consisted of at least ten row homes on each side, but in this particular section of the city, at least sixty percent of the homes were vacant. The vacant homes held the homeless, the abandoned, the degenerates, the throw-aways, or opportunities for quick hits on the pipe or tricks for your fancy.

Knowing the danger, my cousins and I made sure we stayed together in a pack, never really playing with the children that lived around the neighborhood, but minding our own business. We always talked to neighbors when our paths crossed. After all, it always pays to be polite, but it was never more than a simple hello. Still, he caught my eye.

He was the cutest boy I had ever seen. His hair was a black velvet Afro; his slanted eyes were a soft brown. We actually looked more alike than different. Every Sunday, he would walk by my grandmother's home glancing over for what seemed like a million times, and I knew that I had caught his eye too. He was never alone—no one was in this neighborhood—but was always with one or two of his many siblings. It amazed me that his mother, a rather large woman, could have given birth to so many children, for she had more than my grandmother. To me, my grandmother had bred a tribe, whereas Velvet's mother bred a nation. Believe it or not, all of the boys in that family were gorgeous. As a matter of fact, all of the neighborhood girls swooned over them, and Velvet was the quiet one of the bunch. He wasn't into flashy clothes like his brothers. A simple white T-shirt, jeans, and Converse® sneakers were all he wore, but it didn't matter.

Every Sunday, I looked forward to seeing him saunter by my grandmother's house a million times. My cousins caught on to our secret glances, as did his family, and they would eagerly tease both of us about the obvious crush we had on each other. After awhile, we finally had the courage to actually speak to one another with a soft "hi," but it wasn't long before our greetings turned into conversations.

Now instead of walking by, he sat down on the front step, and we talked about things that weren't considered important to anyone but us. His dimples, his smile, and his cool and casual manner left me blushing every time I saw him. I looked forward to every Sunday, and our attendance at church had absolutely nothing to do with it. He didn't go to church as far as I knew, and I couldn't get out of church fast enough to get over to Queen's in order to see my friend.

Week after week, the more time we spent together, the more we talked and got to know each other. We'd walk to the corner store where he'd dig into his pockets and pull out money to buy penny candy. We'd share the usual sweet treats of Mary Janes®, swizzle sticks, Charm lollipops, and Now and Laters. In addition, we always bought the twin Popsicles® that you could split down the middle, turning one Popsicle into two. We were in the same grade, were the same age, and had so much in common it seemed as if we'd known each other forever and would always be friends—until he went away.

He left me on a spring night. The sun had already gone down, as we sat at our usual spot on my grandmother's front step. My cousins were playing all around us, but we didn't seem to notice them. Our attention was focused on a group of girls across the street that had formed their own "Soul Train" line, bumping, hustling, and doing the robot to music blaring from a little transistor radio. We laughed until our bellies ached at their antics and mockery of the popular TV show, until one of his many brothers interrupted our conversation to say another one of his brothers was involved in a fight.

He didn't want to go; I could see it in his face. I didn't want him to go, but he had to—it was expected of him. He flashed his handsome smile, told me he'd be back in a bit, and sauntered off to see what was going on. I watched the two brothers quickly jog away towards the end of the block and disappear around the corner.

When children are engrossed in a game, minutes can turn into an hour. Before they realized how much time has passed, the sun slowly descends on the horizon. I had turned my attention to another group of friends. We ran, jumped, and laughed at ourselves and one another, enjoying our time together.

It wasn't until I heard my mother calling for us to come and get cleaned up before my father arrived to pick us up that I realized how much time had passed—and that Velvet had not returned.

I certainly didn't want to wait another week to see my handsome friend, but my thoughts were interrupted by the screeching sound of the ambulance that roared by. It was not an uncommon sound. This part of the city was always filled with the bellowing of fire engines, police sirens, and the like. But then, two police cars sped by to follow the ambulance that had just turned the corner. My cousins and I looked at each other wondering what had happened. Our questions filled the ghetto night air. Who was being arrested this time? What's going on now? Even some of the neighbors came to their front doors to see what all of the noise was about.

Isn't it strange how eminent danger draws people towards it? It was obvious that something negative had happened, as evidenced by the presence of law enforcement. But, those sirens blaring in the air always seemed to serve as a town crier calling for a city meeting, as opposed to a deterrent to go the opposite direction, drawing crowds in a zombie-like march towards the scene. And we weren't any different.

It was my cousin's idea to investigate, as adults and children started to move toward the commotion. My mother always told me if something bad seemed to be going on, I should head the other way. But I figured if the police were there, whatever was going on couldn't be too bad. After all, they were the law.

Before I could venture towards the commotion, my father's shiny black car pulled up next to the curb, crushing my hopes of hood adventure. I was disgusted to see him. I was angry. Not only was he pulling me away from my cousins, along with dashing my chances of seeing my prince before my departure, I'd have to go home with him. Since he spent his Sunday afternoons drinking, smoking, or God knows what, he was the last person I wanted to be around. But, I didn't have a choice. I was expected to climb into the car, take my rightful seat, and do as I was told. Had I known this day was the last I would ever see Velvet, I'd have insisted that I remain. How can one know what lies in the futuristic tick-tock of the clock?

Still, like everyone else, I had to know what happened. Hood sources shared that while enjoying an innocent game of basketball, someone got angry and tempers flared, as brothas can get if they feel they're being cheated or beaten. A game of basketball—or any game in the hood—not only challenges the participants athletically, but also puts their very manhood on the line. What started as a simple game of basketball, turned into cuss words spit into the air, insults thrown into faces, characters challenged, and pride hurt. The argument had gone too far, as arms started to swing and fists hit their targets.

The fight moved beyond the basketball court and into the street, as more and more people joined the melee. Brothers, cousins, uncles, and those who claimed to be bound by family blood—including my Velvet—had been summoned to fight a fight that really wasn't theirs. No one saw the gun; it was just a basketball game, right? Nothing more than a small disagreement, right? I don't know if anyone even heard the gun go off, but the bullet sailed through the air at lightning speed and found an innocent target—my friend. That one bullet found its way to his chest, and he died in the middle of the street. The black asphalt soaked up the bloody pool that oozed from his chest. The thought of his death was branded in my brain. I could hear the screams and yells of his mother, his angry brothers' pounding of fists against the ground. Whispers and murmurs of fear traveled from one to another as they talked of a senseless death. They held their children tighter that night knowing the bullet could've had anyone's name on it.

Someone I considered a friend, someone I liked and had a crush on had died, and I wasn't sure how I should feel. Not only had he died, but he had been murdered, shot down in the ghetto streets while others huddled around his cold body, gaping and staring at him as if he were road kill waiting to be cleaned up.

When my mother spoke of my friend's death, I needed an answer. I wanted to know why he had to die. I felt that my father could give insight into this tragedy, and I believed that he would help me to understand his senseless death. It was then that he taught another lesson, "That boy had to stand with his brothers. He understood that blood is thicker than water." He then turned to me and told me to never forget that.

Was that the only rationale for my friend losing his life, and, if so, did that justify it? His future was cut short, probably over an argument that meant nothing. The only reason my father could give was to say he had basically done his tour of duty in the hood, stood strong like a soldier next to his brothers, and his medal of honor was a bullet hole to his chest.

For years the death of my friend and the clarity of the moment stayed with me. It was this lesson—blood is thicker than water—that taught me of the bond which should exist in the family unit.

I learned that the family structure has to have a ride-or-die philosophy that must never be broken. I was taught that things occurring within our family were to remain there. All of the secrets, the hurts, and the pain—like tears—were to be locked within our souls because the family bond is the life force that flows within every fiber of our being. It's the blood that acts as the gasoline for the heart, keeping all of us inextricably joined together. If one family member fights, we all fight for him or her, whether we are fond of each other or not. We had to be there for each other, even if it meant death. All for one and one for all.

This lesson holds true throughout the fabric of the family unit, for no matter what, I will forever be bound to my family. My DNA, though uniquely made for me, holds traces of the family from which I came. There are those within a family unit who may disagree and even fall out with one another, but in times of crisis, family will stand with family and beside family.

This great institution of family was created by God. He is the originator of its structure and it is His family—the family of God—where unconditional love can and should be found. However, it can only be found once we are willing to acknowledge that the bond we share goes beyond our DNA, our genetic makeup, and those individual identifiers given by God, such as our fingerprints.

Our bond as children of God exceeds opinions, idiosyncrasies, and points of view, for our Heavenly Father embodies the title of patriarch and matriarch of our family unit. Therefore, everything that occurs within our family must always be done for His glorification, and then for the family's edification.

Of course, family members will not always get along or see things eye to eye. We are family, yet each and every family member is an individual within their own right, with their own opinions and ideas brought about by the various situations and circumstances He allows us to encounter. However, it's our individuality, in conjunction with the special gift that He's instilled within each and everyone one of us, that brings value to the experience of being a part of His family. And it is when we choose to live as He would have us live, use what He has instilled within, and respect what He has given, that His family unit works the way Paul describes as "a body" in Ephesians 4:11-13.

When we are willing to own who we are in Him, then and only then can His family effectively operate as it should. They will touch this world and know, beyond the shadow of each and every doubt, that the children of God are present, but abiding in our Savior.

It was my father's lesson that introduced me to the bond of the family, i.e. blood is truly thicker than water. However, it is the precious blood of the Son of my Father—my Savior—that was shed for me and is not only thicker than water, but reaches further. It has traveled from the foot of Calvary's cross and down the halls of time to meet me in the watery grave of baptism, so that I can be a part of His family—the Family of God and the Church that Jesus built—where I have found the undeniable, unconditional, incomparable, and everlasting love of the resurrected Savior.

Many songs and hymns have been written about His sacrifice on Calvary, but there is one song of long ago that affects me like no other—Andraé Crouch's "The Blood Will Never Lose Its Power":

> The blood that Jesus shed for me,
> Way back on Calvary;
> The blood that gives me strength from day to day,
> It will never lose its' power.
> It reaches to the highest mountain.
> And it flows to the lowest valley.
> The blood that gives me strength from day to day,
> It will never lose its' power.

So, yes, the blood of my father runs through my veins. But, it is the blood of my Savior, the Son of my Father, that allows me to do as the prophet Isaiah suggests in chapter 40, verse 31, to "...mount up with wings as eagles, run and not be weary and to walk and not faint," as I journey toward the home that He has prepared not only for me, but for the family of those that await His coming and look forward to spending eternity with Him.

✾

LESSON FOUR
He Don't Work Like That

If there's one thing I've learned while living in the hood, it's that black people or African-Americans (whichever label is most appealing), as a whole, are a religious group of people. All of my friends attended some type of church somewhere in the hood, and our home wasn't any different.

Because we rose early on Sunday morning, I wasn't allowed to stay up late and play on Saturday, for that time was for the specific purpose of my mother getting everything in order for the Lord's day that approached. That meant that clothes had to be pressed to starched stiffness, bodies had to be bathed, and hair had to be done. My mother believed that those who rushed and hurried themselves, waiting until Sunday morning to take care of these things, were unorganized, slothful, and lazy.

It didn't matter what happened during the week or what transpired that weekend, she made it clear that we were to be in the Lord's house on Sunday morning. Forget the fact that on Saturday, my mother and father might've had a knock-down-drag-out fight. She was going to make it to church—if only to lay her burdens down; I had no choice but to go with her. Not to lay any burden down, mind you, but to lay my head against the most comfortable cushion ever created— the arm of my godmother, a portly woman who was the wife of the preacher and much older than my mother.

This woman and her preacher husband had comforted my mother during her teenage years after her beloved father had passed away, and she was forever grateful to them for their love and acts of kindness during her days of bereavement. They gave her stability when she was looking for an outlet from her responsibilities as the oldest daughter: caring, cooking, and overseeing domestic duties that her mother often was not there to perform. It was for this reason my mother felt a sense of loyalty to these church folk that gathered in a small brick building on the north side of town.

When I opened my eyes in the morning and heard the usual gospel sounds from the radio, confirming that it was indeed Sunday, I made my way to the bathroom to take care of the ritual of personal hygiene. My mother bounced into the room, full of glee and a smile, bearing the good news that my father would be accompanying us to church that day. That really didn't mean anything to me, nor did it hold any special revelation. He always drove us to church on Sunday morning, kept the car so he could do what he wanted, and picked us up at my grandmother's house in the evening. I suppose my lack of enthusiasm or the look on my face spoke of my disinterest, for my mother exclaimed, "He's not dropping us off, he's going to go to church with us!"

I was in shock—to my knowledge, he had never set foot in that church building. I wondered if he even had a suit to wear for the occasion.

My mother was so excited that she grabbed my hands and did a Ring-Around-the-Rosie dance. She told me that our family should be in church together on Sunday mornings, as she pranced around in her slip, singing along with gospel music at the top of her lungs. I was sure the neighbors could hear her rendition of "How I Got Over."

After my mother dressed me, she gave stern instructions for me to sit very still on the couch in our living room, so I wouldn't cause a wrinkle in my perfectly ironed dress. In my mind, there was no way this dress could wrinkle. If anything, it would crack into a million pieces from all the starch she used. Mother always said that ironing was therapeutic for her; she would do it for hours at a time.

Just before my antsiness got the best of me, I saw a man coming down the steps with a black suit, a white shirt, and a black tie. For a moment, I didn't even know who this man was. Then I realized it was my father. He had cleaned up nicely. His everyday construction wear of army green with steel-toed boots was gone, and his hair was smoothed down with a mixture of pomade and water. He even had on shiny, black shoes. I was impressed and smiled brightly at my debonair father. Although, even with his clean, sharp clothes, his face still held a sternness and hardness that was always there.

Upon leaving, our family climbed into my father's shiny black car with the shiny black leather interior. We made our way to the other side of town—the north side—so that we could worship as a family should. During the entire thirty-five minute ride, my mother talked incessantly while my father simply drove. I guess she was unable to contain her excitement, but after a while, I couldn't take her cackling any longer and decided to roll down the window, so that the air could beat on my eardrums, drowning out the forever chatter that flowed from her lips.

My father was never a talkative man. He said what he had to say, and the look on his face almost dared you to ask him to repeat anything. But, he always expected you to listen, follow, and learn from what had been said. He wasn't a loud person, but was often too quiet. It was the sort of quiet that left you wondering what was going through his brain. If he wanted you to know his thoughts, he'd share them; otherwise you were left to wonder.

My mother talked enough for both of them, due to her excitement. Even when my father parked the car and turned off the ignition, her mouth continued to run like an engine. She didn't stop talking until we walked through the red door of the shout-'til-you-pass-out church building which was nothing more than a renovated row home that sat on the corner. Its only designation as a holy place was a small sign posted in the window and the red door. Red was the color of all church doors in our city, I suppose by city mandate.

The walls that once separated the living room from the dining room and kitchen on the first floor of this used-to-be home were knocked out, making one big room. Wooden folding chairs were arranged in rows from one wall to the other. At the front of the room were two wooden pews. Directly in front of the pews was a small carpeted wooden stage, complete with a wooden pulpit. On the right wall, an old piano faced the window. Beyond the sanctuary was a small kitchen which was left intact. The dark, damp basement held the unisex bathroom. I hated that basement. I hated all basements. They were scary places, and I'd rather hold my pee than go down there to release it.

Like my mother, I, too, was excited that my father had decided to join us for church that Sunday, and I was hopeful that everyone would like him. I knew they couldn't deny his sharp and clean outward appearance, but sometimes people can be so judgmental, tending to eye a person and come to a conclusion before words are even exchanged. Regardless of who thought what, no one could wipe the smile from my mother's face as we entered that little shout-'til-you-pass-out church building on that Sunday morning.

There couldn't have been more than thirty people gathered there that day, which was the usual attendance, but you would've thought there were at least one hundred by the volume of singing, the tambourines shaking, and the piano playing. Folks shouted, whooped, and hollered as if they were at a concert. In the midst of the singing, my mother, in her pride and glory, swished her way to the front, thinking that my father would follow her lead, but he lingered in the back. This was all new to him, I suppose, so he felt the need to check out what he had walked into before placing himself in front of the congregation.

I slowly walked over to my godmother and turned to see where my father was going to sit, when I was met with his urging look to go on and sit down. As I assumed my usual position, with a once-in-a-while glance to see if my father was okay, the whooping, hollering, tambourine beating, and piano playing turned into a dull lullaby in my ears. My usual routine took over—my head nestled into my godmother's cushiony arm.

Those folk must've sung for over an hour. Song after song, hymn after hymn, holler after holler, until finally, the preacher stood as a mountain before us on the platform, his deep baritone voice filling the room. He was a rather large man. Every Sunday, it seemed like his stomach had grown to where you'd think he was carrying a grown man inside. I never understood what he was saying, but my mother claimed that he was a powerful preacher. Powerfully big. Every week, his words just lulled me right off to sleep against my godmother's arm. Knowing the preacher's tendency to be long-winded, I figured on a good hour or so nap.

That was not to be the case on this particular Sunday, for as I was sleeping good, dreaming about who knows what, suddenly someone let out a yell that woke me up. Chairs were being turned over, and my godmother sat me upright before making her way to the front.

I had been told this is what happens when somebody catches the Holy Spirit. A few women locked their arms together, forming a tight circle around a woman while her body was flailing every which way. Her head flopped from side to side and her feet moved like she was jumping double-dutch, while it appeared she was trying to break free from the encircled lockdown. This wasn't uncommon in the shout-'til-you-pass-out church. I had seen this happen to women and men on many occasions, but did it have to interrupt my good nap?

As the three women continued their tight lockdown of the

woman, probably to protect the rest of the building from her antics, someone else yelled. This time it was the preacher. I guess he'd caught the Holy Spirit, too. How he caught it, I don't know. Did she toss it over to him? Did it attack him? Whatever way he caught it, the preacher started jumping up and down like a pogo stick. He wasn't flailing around like the woman; he just went straight up and down in that little square pulpit area. "Boom! Boom! Boom!" The sound echoed in the small space every time his feet connected with the floor of the platform, due to his massive weight.

My mother had made her way up front to see if she could help my godmother and the other women, who seemed to be struggling with the rag doll woman, and I turned around to see what my father thought of all this. He was gone. He wasn't in his seat anymore.

I wondered where he had gone, but my thoughts were interrupted by a loud crash. When I turned around to see the source of the crashing sound, the preacher's body had fallen through the floor up to his giant globe of a waist.

Immediately, the room was quiet and still. The pianist wasn't playing, the tambourines were hushed, the rag doll woman stood stark still. Everyone stopped dancing, prancing, yelling, and screaming. At first, no one knew what to do, and no one moved. You could've heard a pin drop. Suddenly, one of the men jumped to attention while other men followed to help pull their fallen preacher out of the floor. The wooden platform had evidently split under the weight of his jumping up and down, and his fat legs were dangling through the basement ceiling. Those men huffed and puffed to pull their preacher out of the hole he had created. Maybe a crane would have been more effective.

By the time they finally freed him from the hole in the floor/basement ceiling, he was drenched in sweat, as were those who had pulled him out. The adults rushed over to him to make sure their preacher was OK. All of the children—me included—slowly made our way to the platform and stood there with our mouths hanging open, as we peered into the crater-sized open hole.

Needless to say, the church service came to an abrupt end as we filed out of the little brick building. I wondered if this was really the work of the Holy Spirit, and, if so, what made Him leave so fast, because no one claimed to have caught Him for a long time after that.

I couldn't wait to tell my father about what had happened and found him leaning against his black, shiny car smoking a cigarette.

I told him of the events from start to finish and asked if that's what happens when the Holy Spirit shows up. He never looked at me, but simply tilted his head back, closed his eyes, and let out a long drag of smoke before answering. This was yet another lesson to be learned, though it was spoken with few words, as he replied, "He don't work like that."

I can never judge the heart, soul, and mind of another human being. I was not created for that purpose, and I believe that God is the only one that can judge such matters.

As a child attending this shout-'til-you-pass-out church, I was encouraged to shout and to tarry for the Holy Spirit. I was instructed that tarrying is a way in which we invite the Holy Spirit to enter our lives, so that He will fill us with His power. Tarrying, as it was explained to me, included an individual pouring out of one's soul on the altar of prayer while the person chanted over and over again as an invitation of some sort, as well as a show of sincerity, so that the Holy Spirit would finally make Himself known in your life. Once the Holy Spirit decided to make His appearance in your life, it was evident by your physical response to His presence. This response included speaking in an unknown tongue, passing out, and falling backwards, including twitching or shouting, not of a verbal nature, but a prance of sorts. If you did any of these things, you had indeed been successful in catching the Holy Spirit.

I witnessed many occasions where men and women claimed to receive the Holy Spirit. Some ran laps around the building, rolled around on the floor, danced on top of pianos, did cartwheels, and even spoke in this unknown language that I was told only the Holy Spirit—not even God—could understand.

Is this the result of a confrontation and encounter with the Holy Spirit? Does this constitute worship? Again, I cannot speak for those who truly believe that their experience was what it was. I can only speak where the Bible speaks and be silent where it is silent. John, one of Christ's disciples, the dirty dozen, records the account of Christ meeting a Samaritan woman in John 4. The Savior tells her in verse 24:

> God is a Spirit and those that worship Him must worship Him in spirit and in truth.

As His child, and with Him as my Father, I must be willing to acknowledge that the Bible is the inspired Word of God. His Word contains the manual, handbook, guidelines, and standard operating procedures for how children of God should conduct themselves and how His Kingdom, the Church, should be organized. These inspired words give comfort when needed, chastisement when necessary, confirmation of His promises, calm in the midst of a storm, and direction as we journey from earth to glory and speak of the celestial shores of heaven that await those who are faithful to Him.

Before the Savior's departure and return back to glory, He instructs His disciples to wait or tarry for the Comforter, the Holy Spirit. He tells them in John 16:7-16:

> Nevertheless I tell you the truth; It is expedient for you that I go away: for if I go not away, the Comforter will not come unto you; but if I depart, I will send him unto you.
>
> [8]And when he is come, he will reprove the world of sin,

and of righteousness, and of judgment:

⁹Of sin, because they believe not on me;

¹⁰Of righteousness, because I go to my Father, and ye see me no more;

¹¹Of judgment, because the prince of this world is judged.

¹²I have yet many things to say unto you, but ye cannot bear them now.

¹³Howbeit when he, the Spirit of truth, is come, he will guide you into all truth: for he shall not speak of himself; but whatsoever he shall hear, that shall he speak: and he will shew you things to come.

¹⁴He shall glorify me: for he shall receive of mine, and shall shew it unto you.

¹⁵All things that the Father hath are mine: therefore said I, that he shall take of mine, and shall shew it unto you.

¹⁶A little while, and ye shall not see me: and again, a little while, and ye shall see me, because I go to the Father.

The Savior then tells His disciples where they are to go in order to receive the Comforter in Luke 24:46-52:

⁴⁶And said unto them, Thus it is written, and thus it behooved Christ to suffer, and to rise from the dead the third day:

⁴⁷And that repentance and remission of sins should be preached in his name among all nations, beginning at Jerusalem.

⁴⁸And ye are witnesses of these things.

⁴⁹And, behold, I send the promise of my Father upon you: but tarry ye in the city of Jerusalem, until ye be endued with power from on high.

⁵⁰And he led them out as far as to Bethany, and he lifted up his hands, and blessed them.

⁵¹And it came to pass, while he blessed them, he was parted from them, and carried up into heaven.

⁵²**And they worshipped him, and returned to Jerusalem with great joy:**

In obeying the Savior, Christ's disciples went to the city of Jerusalem, and Peter preaches a powerful sermon, resulting in the baptism of three thousand souls. However, it is Peter's words which confirm that by believing, repenting of sins, confessing that Christ is Lord, and being baptized, we receive the gift of the Holy Spirit in Acts 2:38:

> ³⁸**Then Peter said unto them, Repent, and be baptized every one of you in the name of Jesus Christ for the remission of sins, and ye shall receive the gift of the Holy Ghost.**

The Holy Spirit is received at the very moment that we are baptized into the family of God. We no longer have to wait for His appearance or be on the lookout for Him. He is with us, abiding within and guiding us into all truths.

Paul, in his letter to the church at Corinth, further informs us that the Spirit dwells within in I Corinthians 3:16-17:

> ¹⁶**Know ye not that ye are the temple of God, and that the Spirit of God dwelleth in you?**
> ¹⁷**If any man defile the temple of God, him shall God destroy; for the temple of God is holy, which temple ye are.**

The Holy Spirit is a living and breathing personality of the Trinity—the Father, the Son and the Holy Spirit. They are three in one. They coexist and you can't have one without the other.

What a blessing to know that my Father has given me all that is required to live a life that is pleasing to Him. He is my Father, His Son is my Savior, and His Spirit is my Comforter. This is evident in my communication with Him, for prayer is the avenue whereby I am able to talk with Him any time and any place.

During prayer, my gratitude, requests, praise, and petitions are filtered through the Son, my mediator (I Timothy 2:5), for only He can express to the Father my inner thoughts and feelings. He alone experienced what it means to live on this planet called earth. My Savior tells me that my prayers are directed to my Father (Matthew 6:9), and it is the Holy Spirit that bears witness of my spirit during my prayer (Romans 8:16).

What a joy to know that I have the CIA—Christ's Inner Alliance—the Father, the Son and the Holy Spirit, working on my behalf all hours of the day and night for the lifetime that He has given to me and working on behalf of all those that are His.

LESSON FIVE
Keep Your Hands To Yourself

I believe it's during the toddler age when children tend to take on a possessive nature where they stake out their own territory. With a dogmatic tenaciousness, they will grasp, pull, and cling to whatever they feel belongs to them.

You often hear toddlers' shouts over and over again, as they strive to inform others that what they have—a blanket, a bottle, or even something as minute as a bubblegum wrapper—belongs solely to them and should not be touched by anyone else. Any attempts to remove the item they feel truly belongs to them results in the bellowing anthem "It's mine!" and may be accompanied by kicks, screams, and tantrums.

Older children, teenagers, and even adults seem to forget the phrase "It's mine!", but it teaches us of wanting to be in possession of something that we can call our own. However, sometimes, children, wanting to claim things for themselves, will cross the line and the boundaries set in place. They will reach out and grab, or latch on to, something that was in the possession of another and claim it for their own, prompting adults to sing their own anthem, "Keep your hands to yourself." In other words, don't touch what doesn't belong to you.

Apparently, this lesson only applied to children, because when children become adults, some of them will steal, abuse, rip off, hoodwink, hustle, and con one another. Perhaps their actions are a psychological regaining of independence, quenching the inner child's desire that cries "It's mine!" or simply because they never fully grasped the lesson of keeping your hands to yourself. Maybe they didn't even care enough to respect other people's property. However, this lesson was taught under completely different circumstances with different results by my father.

Our city, like most major cities, was full of people that had come upon hard times. Sometimes, life just happens, and despite a person's best efforts, it's not enough, considering the obstacles. We would ride along in the hood, and from time to time, there would be a person standing on the corner or camped out at an intersection holding a sign or a cup, asking for assistance. I've seen some children make fun of these people, looking at them in a degrading way, as if their existence were a blot on human society, but my mother taught me that to ridicule these people was wrong, and I was careful not to do that.

These weren't the usual hood winos. Everyone knew the hood wino, and rarely did they ask for anything. The hood winos seemed happy and content to sit or lay there on the sidewalk, as long as they had their brown paper bag which held a choice bottle of sweet nectar. The hood winos never asked for any help and would sometimes share their sidewalk philosophy with you. They always knew what was goin' on in the hood, because no one ever paid attention to them listening and looking. But, they knew what to reveal, when to reveal it, and who to reveal or not reveal things to.

However, these advertising, cup-holding people never lived in the hood. As a matter of fact, I don't know where they came from, but they were always there, waiting on the outskirts and boundaries of the hood, hoping to get a nickel, dime, quarter or money that crinkles, as opposed to the kind that jingles.

They were poorly dressed, with clothes full of holes resembling the too-much-dirt-to-get-clean look. Shoes were holey, if they had them on, and hair was unruly. Some of these people held up signs scribbled with the words, "Will work for food." I wondered who would hire someone that didn't even have shoes to wear?

If you were driving your car and ended up being stopped at a red light, sometimes a person or two or three would materialize out of nowhere holding a squirt bottle and a dirty rag to begin washing your windows, hoping for a tip for the unrequested duty.

I believe the reason I never saw these people in my hood was because they didn't have a home to live in, and chances were they knew they wouldn't receive any type of assistance in our neighborhood. People were too busy trying to handle their own business, feeding the mouths that lived under their roofs, and trying to make their own ends meet.

Homeless people often perched under overpasses, where occasionally there were cardboard boxes fashioned into tents and homes. For some, the grassy lawns of parks became their beds, and branches were used as blankets. If these destitute people had any possessions, they were piled high into a stolen, borrowed, or donated shopping cart. Some even broke into abandoned or vacant row houses to shield them from inclement weather. However, an empty row house could be more than a dry, yet cold, place to lay your head. It was often the meeting place for drug-addicted people looking for a quiet place to purchase and get their high on, dish out sexual favors in exchange for a quick high, or even hide from the law.

When I'd see these people pushing around their worldly possessions or standing at corners for handouts, I often wondered what happened to bring about their demise. Did they ever have a place of employment? Where was their family? Of course, none of these questions were ever answered because I never came close enough to verbally communicate with anyone who was down on their luck—except one day when my father and I were sent to purchase dinner for our family.

It was one of those days when my mother was in need of a break from her domestic duties to which my father reluctantly, though under duress, volunteered to fetch dinner for his family. I never turned down the opportunity to go anyplace—whether for a ride, a walk, a run, or just simply to go—so I gladly accepted the responsibility as co-dinner fetcher.

We hopped into my father's shiny, black car with the leather bucket seats and made our way to find dinner. Despite his sometimes eerie and quiet nature, or my inability to totally relax in his presence, there were times, such as this, that I truly enjoyed being with my father. I could always tell when it was "okay" to be around him, based on the sound of his steps or the look of his stroll. If his footsteps were quick, then he was too focused to be bothered. If his hand was in his pocket, and he was jingling the money inside, he was not to be bothered because the wheels were turning in his mind. On the flipside, if his footsteps were heavy and slow, he was more approachable. If his stroll was laid back, then all was well. On this day, all was good.

On days such as this, he turned on the radio and the deep bass hum filled the car. During these times, he pleasantly asked and quizzed me on lessons he previously taught, kindly reprimanded me if I forgot certain aspects, and even shared updates on his business transactions—legal and illegal. He rarely looked directly at me, being careful to keep his eyes on the road ahead, and, as we drove, he'd eventually ask what my thoughts were for dinner.

My first response was usually a hoagie. A one-of-a-kind sandwich that will never be duplicated. In my travels, I've been introduced to second-class imitations, referred to as submarine sandwiches or subs for short, and even third-class sandwiches that had the audacity to be labeled hoagies. But, the only place to get the original hoagie and truly appreciate it, is in the best delis in the nation, located in our city, where the aromas of imported cheeses, meats, spices, and fresh-baked breads merge and hit your nose at the door, causing the palate to immediately water.

My favorite hoagie was an Italian hoagie. A long, Italian roll, filled with ham, Genoa salami, prosciutto, mortadella, sharp provolone cheese, sweet peppers, and sliced kosher pickles, lightly bathed in an oil-and-vinegar combination. Of course, this delicacy could be made according to personal specifications, but I believed my version was second to none. Plus, a hoagie wasn't complete unless accompanied by the famous Herr potato chips on the side or tucked neatly within the folds of the meat of your hoagie, adding a wonderful crunch with each bite. Hoagies to me were manna from heaven.

If a hoagie was my first choice, then a cheesesteak was my second. It depended on the taste buds, for while the hoagie was cold, the cheesesteak was a hot sandwich. It consisted of a long, Italian roll filled with paper-thin, shaved steak that's been chopped and cooked on the grill with melted American cheese (extra for me) and bathed in ketchup, mustard, and pickles. Some people also like fried onions, peppers, and mayo, or substitute chopped chicken for the steak, but I believe my version was the best. This sandwich is so famous that television food shows have shown battles between various cheesesteak restaurants who continue to boast that theirs is the best.

However, this day, my father vetoed my number one and number two choices. He decided to go with what was usually my third choice—fried chicken. I can truly say that I love fried chicken. Though it was my third choice, my body had to digest fried chicken at least once or twice a week, with the other days going to my other favorites.

In the hood, a chicken can be cooked many ways, which is why there's always such an abundance of it. You can't seem to go wrong with it. Whether it's boiled, stewed, barbecued, baked, or grilled—frying being the best—you can't mess it up. There's no better part of the gospel bird than its wing. A three-jointed piece that is considered white meat, packs more flavor than any other part. Give me a wing, and I'm good to go. I ate so many chicken wings that my father told me I'd soon grow my own and fly away, which might not have been a bad idea considering where we lived.

So, we made our way to the fast-food establishment where we could purchase enough fried chicken and side orders to feed an army. Once my father parked his car, I placed my little hand into his massive claw and tried to keep up with his broad stride. He was a tall man, and, in order for me to keep up, I had to stop walking and pretend to long jump. I jumped over puddles, played imaginary games of counting my steps before stepping on the lines etched in the sidewalk—which wasn't easy given the massive number of cracks—and held onto his hand for support while making our way to the fast-food place.

He swung the door open, and I followed behind him. He was never into chivalry, holding a door for his lady. To him, it was about protection and going before the female to make sure that all was well before allowing her to enter. My father surveyed the restaurant, nodded to those who may have been acquaintances or were simply taking notice, and then made his way to the counter where he placed his order. He ordered so quickly and so much chicken that the girl had trouble keeping up with the words that spilled out of his mouth. But, he was never one to repeat himself, so when she questioningly looked up to him to ensure what she had was correct, he simply nodded his head, paid for the food, and waited to receive the order.

They gave us two big bags full of food and drinks, and I carried another big bag full of biscuits and packets of honey. It was a heavy bag, but I was content to deal with my load, compared to the bags my father held, which seemed as tall as me.

Arriving at the restaurant, I was engrossed in the task at

hand and neglected to take notice of things around me. When we exited, I saw the worst-looking man next to the door entrance.

I think he was a Caucasian male, but the dirt on his face was so heavy he easily could have been an African-American or a Latino with a light complexion—only he and the dirt knew for sure. His hair was hidden under a dirty skull cap, and he had on layered, tattered, soiled, and urine-soaked clothes that looked ten sizes too large. On his feet were a pair of bo bos—off-brand, no-name sneakers. His toes were sticking out through the tip where the material had pulled away from the sole. He was sitting there in his filth, as he held up his skeleton of a hand, while he opened his mouth full of decaying teeth and asked for food. He didn't ask for money, he didn't even say he was hungry; he said he was "so hungry."

I was sure that my father had seen him, for he took note of everything, but I had not noticed him before our departure. Something about him pulled at my heartstrings, as I stood in the doorway in front of him and slowly reached into my big bag of biscuits. He needed help. He needed food, and I had more than enough to spare. My heart hurt for him. I had never been so close to someone like this before. I'd only seen them in passing as I sat behind a car window, and, though the stench kept me at bay, I still wanted to help with a biscuit or two. He didn't scare me, and all of my questions of how he came to be what he was bounced around in my head, but I didn't ask them. I simply reached into my bag for a buttery biscuit to offer this poor man.

Before I could even get my hand out of the bag, my arm was grabbed so hard, I thought my shoulder was pulled from its socket. My father, while holding his two bags in one arm, seized the bag of biscuits from my grasp, and pushed me further away from this man in the direction of our car. He nudged me to walk in front of him, perhaps keeping himself between me and the degenerate man, as the distance between us grew wider and wider, and his chances of receiving some nourishment in the form of a biscuit grew slimmer and slimmer. My father's footsteps were quick and sure.

When we arrived at the car, he placed the bags on the floorboard behind the driver's side, and I jumped in silently. I wanted to know what I did wrong for the anger on his face was evident.

All of the pleasantries from our earlier ride were gone as I told him, "He was hungry." In silence, my father started the engine, and pulled away from the curb without fastening his seat belt. In those days, we never fastened them, nor was the use of them enforced. As we drove away, I kept my eyes cast downward waiting for his response which didn't come until we were blocks away.

"Keep your hands to yourself. You hear me? You don't help nobody but your own, and before you help the people under your roof, you help yourself first. Get your own and don't give away what you got, that's how you lose it," my father said.

He never raised his voice, but his lesson was shared firmly with an even tone. He told me how "those folk" just want to drain you dry, how they're not good for nothin', and that selfishness was really a good thing. He said that they could do better—they just didn't want to. It's not our job to take our hard-earned money and waste it on them. He shared with me how important it is to gather what you make and keep it to yourself—whether it is material or even the lessons he shared—because if you give it away, you'll never get it back.

He said that his lessons were only for his family and again stressed the need to be selfish in all things when it came to helping others. Sometimes, it was even okay to help a good neighbor, but those were usually instances where things were exchanged. For instance, if a cup of flour is borrowed, the following week I may have to borrow a cup of sugar. It's an even trade, and, in those instances, the rules and his lesson didn't apply, but even then you had to be wary of over-extending your hospitality. To him, it was OK to help family because blood is thicker than water, and family has to look out for family and have each other's back. But even then, you have to keep your hands to yourself.

I was never able to grasp this lesson. I never agreed with it. I find that though my tears had been frozen inside for years, as mentioned in previous chapters, my compassion, sympathy, and empathy for those in pain, hurting, and in need, never diminished.

My heart, unlike my father's, was not cold, perhaps because I had not lived his life or lived long enough to be as cold. My heart had not experienced the life he had, though it was touched by it. Yet, in being touched and taught by my father, my heart grew and yearned for what he shunned—to love and to feel. So, in seeing this degenerate man, with whom I'd never come into contact with and had not even noticed prior to my departure from the place of business, my heart was open to his need.

Everyone needs something—whether that thing is of a material nature, emotional, mental, or physical. The human spirit cries out for the fulfillment of that need, and if that need is not filled, people will find ways to fill it. If it is filled and taken away, they will forever search for it. Some even become desperate enough to hurt others in the process of finding it. Over time, when someone goes without something for so long, they become immune to not having it and may even tell themselves they don't need it. In reality, there is a longing and yearning within that never goes away until the thirst is quenched and satisfied.

It is my Father, who has taught me, been the example of and shown me one of the most important lessons that coincides with being His child. To love and to serve. Were it not for the love of my Father, the servitude of His Son, and the inspiration of His Spirit, who have loved me and met each of my needs, I would not be here today. In turn, how can I deny anyone of the gift I've been given? How can I selfishly pass those in need without so much as a wayward glance? How could I dare to be touched, and then not act upon the touch of the Father to reach out to this lost and dying world, where many have yet to understand and encounter His love?

Who am I to imitate those that are portrayed as stepping over, stepping aside, and stepping around the wounded in the parable of the Good Samaritan? Have I not been blessed to bless others? Of course, people say that opening your heart to those in need also opens them up to being used and abused, and even conned. However, along with our blessings and our ability to aid and help those in need, we are also given the insight and wisdom to do so.

In today's society, people are wary of picking up hitchhikers, and rightly so. Our world causes us to think twice before lending a hand to a passerby on the street, and rightly so. We have learned that there are those who ask for monetary gifts, under the guise of being in need of food, only to turn around and feed their daily drug habits, causing us to curtail our giving. In those cases, we must be ever so careful not to be taken advantage of.

However, as His child, because He is my Father, isn't it possible to meet the specific need instead of placing a band-aid over the open wound? If someone cries for food, then supply food. If someone is in need of a ride, call a cab. If approached for money, ask what the money will be used for and supply the specific need, if reasonable.

Our Savior tells us in Matthew 25:35-40:

> For I was hungry, and ye gave me meat: I was thirsty, and ye gave me drink: I was a stranger, and ye took me in:
>
> 36Naked, and ye clothed me: I was sick, and ye visited me: I was in prison, and ye came unto me.

[37]Then shall the righteous answer him, saying, Lord, when saw we thee hungry, and fed thee? or thirsty, and gave thee drink?

[38]When saw we thee a stranger, and took thee in? or naked, and clothed thee?

[39]Or when saw we thee sick, or in prison, and came unto thee?

[40]And the King shall answer and say unto them, Verily I say unto you, inasmuch as ye have done it unto one of the least of these my brethren, ye have done it unto me.

My Father has taught me to bless those because He blessed me, to lend a hand to those because He reached out and grabbed me, and to share His goodness with others because He has certainly been good to me. Anything else, as His child, would be uncivilized.

My mentor uses a quote spoken by Peggy Tabor Millin:

We never touch people so lightly that we do not leave a trace.

These words hold an undeniable truth, for I believe when we choose to act or not to act, we are still felt—either positively or negatively. One of the strongest memories we possess is how we were made to feel. Our attitude is spoken physically, as well as verbally, and people will never care how much you know until they see how much you care. Abandonment, abuse, ignoring, forsaking, betrayal—all of these are feelings that are forever etched in our minds and in our hearts. It's only the love of God that can heal our pain because His love surpasses all of them.

I can talk all day long of the love of God and how He has changed my life, but if I'm unwilling to put His love into action then my words are simply words without meaning. If I sit in my self-assigned seat on Sunday morning, dressed to the nines, sing the songs of Zion, voice an occasional "amen," extend the right hand of fellowship to my church family, but then walk out of that same building with my nose in the air and use that same right hand to slap and shoo away those who need Him most, then my worship is in vain.

My Father taught me that because His touch changed my life, then I, in turn, must reach out and touch somebody's hand to make this world a better place—because I can.

LESSON SIX
You Gotta Make Your Own Way

We moved into our neighborhood when I was barely one year old. At the time, it was a predominantly white neighborhood, but as more and more black folks moved in, "white flight" went into action.

I've been told that's the term used when those of the Caucasian race quickly move from a neighborhood because they don't want to have to live among black people or any other race. And these Caucasian families move with lightning speed, as if they fear a plague or a deadly disease that will overtake them should they choose to remain.

When these neighborhoods take on a different flavor, going from vanilla to chocolate, some of them adopting the term "chocolate city," sometimes the property value goes down because a change takes place. It's no longer called a neighborhood, it's called a hood. The broken lives that occupy the broken homes are evident from inside out as broken beer bottles litter the streets and the broken sidewalks. It's almost as if those that live there have lost their pride or never had it to begin with, so they don't know it's missing and don't even try to look for it.

There are some neighborhoods in the ghetto that take pride in being there by putting neighborhood watch organizations in place. It's in these neighborhoods that the occupants sweep up and keep it clean, but sometimes, instilling pride is not always easy to do. It's not easy to make people take care of what they have.

As stated in a previous chapter, most homes in the hood are single parent homes. The mother, the usual single parent, does what she can to make ends meet. She takes care of her children, her home and herself, but it can be a difficult challenge—especially if jobs are scarce and the only person that single mother can depend on is herself.

If the single mother's children respect her, as they grow, they will do what they can to assist—even if that means borrowing, hustling, or stealing.

In our home, having a mother and a father was a rarity. Even more rare was the fact that not only was there a mother and a father living under the same roof and occupying the same space, but they were also married. They weren't shacking up, they didn't have a common law marriage, nor did they play house. They actually had a ceremony where my mother wore a just-below-the-knee white wedding dress, white shoes, and a white veil. My father's attire was a pressed, black suit; shiny, black shoes; and a white shirt with a bow tie. He even slicked his hair back for the occasion—probably with that thick pomade in the orange metal can I'd seen him use.

I can only imagine them looking into each other's eyes, saying "'til death do us part," and some years later wishing or praying that the parting would come sooner than the dying. My parents had been married a little less than one year before I came along. Not long after moving into our new home, my father decided to step outside of the invisible, yet definite, ghetto boundaries put in place by those who had departed and start his very own construction business.

Because of this business we didn't have to scrounge, scrape, and struggle to make ends meet. My parents didn't have to beat the pavements for work or worry about making it from paycheck to paycheck. We were able to buy whatever we wanted when we wanted it.

My mother didn't even have to work. She could stay home all day long, watch her soap operas, keep our house clean, and have meals ready for our arrival, just as my father wanted it to be.

He felt that with his business, which he named after both of them in order to give her some sort of input, his wife shouldn't and wouldn't have to work. I used to believe this was a privilege, but as I grew older, I learned it was nothing more than a means of control. Money was never scarce, and I never gave much thought to it. I was simply a child lookin' for love, having fun, and enjoying the hood life. I only wanted to play, laugh, and eat. I didn't even give much thought to where I laid my head, as long as I was with my family. Because I was the only child for quite some time, I became used to being the center of my parents' world.

I was what some would consider spoiled. If I wanted it, I got it. If this is the definition of being spoiled, then so be it. But, I never saw it that way. I always understood someone being spoiled as an individual who is used to getting his or her way—no matter who it hurts or harms, regardless if it's an imposition. The spoiled one could care less who it offends. Getting my way was never done so at the expense of another. I just wanted what I wanted when I wanted it, and for me, it was simply love defined.

I believed that my father's routine weekend excursions taking me to the toy store was because he loved me and wanted to make me happy. It never dawned on me it was a ludicrous tradition, even when I cried, because I already had every toy that was in the store. I understood our weekly excursion was because my father had grown up on a poor farm in the south, and, now that he had his own money, he never wanted his family to want for anything. He was going to make a way to provide for us.

We ate out at least two or three times a week, giving my mother a break from her domestic duties. We had always had two or three cars and a truck. The house was nicely furnished. We were always nicely dressed. Was I spoiled? I don't know; I just saw it as the way it was supposed to be.

Of course, my mother borrowed the cup of sugar or flour here and there from neighbors and vice versa, but it was never because we couldn't afford it. She was simply out of it and didn't want to take the time to go or send me to the store to get what was needed.

Money flowed freely in our home, and our extended family would often pull their hands out of empty pockets looking for a loan, grant, or some benevolent measure. Most times those empty pockets were filled without the expectation of being paid back.

The tough times that other families in the neighborhood were having didn't seem to affect us—until later when my parents' business fell on hard times. After becoming used to the luxuries that come with consistent money, the dip in pay, shift in dollars, or lack of loot caused my father to search out other ways to provide for his family.

He found what he considered to be the perfect way to make ends meet, but didn't tell my mother what it was. I don't know where he came up with the idea. I don't know if it was introduced to him, or if he conjured it up in his own mind, but pretty soon it was evident that he had a new gig going.

In a matter of days, my father and our home became a popular spot in the neighborhood, as we received visitors on a regular basis. Some of them I knew from the hood, some I didn't, but they became a constant stream. At first, the occasional stranger at the front door didn't seem unusual; however, in a matter of time, the now-and-then doorbell became a constant ring from early evening until sunrise.

I never asked my mother if she knew why we had this sudden influx of people; she seemed oblivious to it. But, the doorbell had to go. At the urging of my mother, my father disconnected the doorbell because once he came home, it was a constant drone as he spent more time during his non-working hours on our enclosed porch.

He would sit there in a chair eating watermelon, sipping on an ice-cold Pepsi, or watching the television he placed out there, so he could see people approach, meet them at the door, and handle his business.

As business grew, so did my curiosity. For some reason, when adults do things, they don't seem to realize that children are aware of what they're doing. Perhaps the adults are operating under the reasoning that children are too young to notice, don't pay attention, or are too young to understand. This is true and untrue. It's untrue because children are the best observers. That's how they learn. Children absorb everything they see and everything they hear, whether the adult is able to acknowledge it or not. It's true that though children see and hear, their ability to fully comprehend what they see and hear is based on a yet-to-mature mind.

In witnessing and taking note of what I saw, I didn't fully understand the actions at the time. But, I had to know why, when someone ventured up our front steps, my father would stand in the doorway, whispering. I had to know why the person stayed on the steps and never ventured inside, while my father hustled to the kitchen. I longed to know why upon his return, the person on the other side of the door exchanged hands with my father and walked away, while my father shoved his hands deep in his pockets.

And so it was, while receiving a steady stream of guests, my curiosity encouraged me to follow him to the kitchen, in order to understand what I had witnessed, being careful to keep my distance as he made his transaction.

He was so busy handling his business that he didn't even notice me standing there watching him, after he had gone to the kitchen and reached into the cabinet under the kitchen sink. He simply breezed by and made his usual way to the front door, as I stood staring at the cabinet.

I knew that if I wanted to know what kept him moving from the front door to the kitchen and back, my time was limited, because at any minute, my father would hurry this way. I had to act and act fast.

Quickly and quietly, I crept into the kitchen, knelt down on the floor directly in front of the cabinet underneath the sink, and opened the door. The roach that scurried across the floorboard just inches away, caused me to jump back in fright. I always hated those things. No matter how many of them you killed, and even if I was one hundred times larger, they were nasty little creatures, and the death of one resulted in the reincarnation of one million more.

As the roach disappeared into the cracks under the cabinet, not wanting to get too close for fear that the roach's brother would suddenly appear, I looked inside. I could see them. What looked like hundreds of them. Stacked neatly in rows and piles on top of each other. Small, clear plastic bags with different colored pills inside. Other plastic bags with what looked like oregano in them. Cigarette wrapper paper. Some bags with rolled up cigarettes. More bags with plastic vials inside of them. I knew what it meant. I now knew why people were coming to the front door in droves.

I became so engrossed looking at the bags that I never heard my father. I never saw him. I did feel his rough hands grab me from behind, throw me into the air, and pin me against the kitchen wall. My little legs dangled, my eyes were full of fear, unfallen tears were frozen deep inside threatening to escape, and my chest wanted to cave in from the pressure of his hand.

"Whatchu doin'?" he said. Before I could even think to answer, he gave me a warning to steer away from the cabinet underneath the kitchen, forget what I saw, and keep my mouth shut. That meant my mother definitely didn't know what he was doing and couldn't hear it from me. He needed to hear that I would promise to do what he said. In a barely audible whisper, I struggled to tell him I would. He allowed me to drop to the floor, reached for what he came for under the sink, and stormed back to another patron that waited at the front door.

My father had become the keeper of crack. A street pharmacist. A drug dealer, and business was booming, making his previous business look like a bubble gum machine. He was making so much money he had to hire more and more people to keep business flowing. All roads led to our home as neighbors, friends, relatives, and strangers came looking to escape the funk of city life by ignoring reality or easing the pain of their existence.

My father was always careful not to allow the patrons to enter our home. That was off limits. After awhile, his gig had to find another central location, in order to protect his family, his nest, and the place where he was supposed to lay his head. He purchased a garage less than a mile away and used it as a front to dispense his addictive candy. It was raided many times, yet he never spent a night in jail.

From his "auto body shop," he furnished corner after corner with his products, reaching one side of the city to the other and beyond state lines, and still, he went untouched. Men, women, boys, and girls looked upon him as the Robin Hood of the ghetto—even though lives were changed, families were destroyed, and lives were lost as a result of his dealings. Still, he found great pleasure in being the deliverer of death.

He couldn't see beyond the money, the benjamins, and the stacks of rubber-banded cash enough to care. As far as he was concerned, it was a means to an end, and he had every intention of seeing it through to the end.

As a child, it never phased me. As a teenager, it intrigued me. As a young adult, it captivated me. But, as an adult, it haunted me.

I had so many questions I had never thought to ask. I wanted to know if he had regrets. I needed to know if it bothered him that lives had been lost. I wondered if he ever lost sleep at night. I had hundreds of questions that only he could answer, but as I sat next to him one summer evening, they left my mind and escaped my memory. All I could think to give was my dissertation on the illegality of selling drugs. I tried to impress upon him how playing this game of Russian roulette would eventually catch up with him, even though it hadn't for twenty-plus years. I didn't want him to think that I was being judgmental. After all, he was my father and because of his lucrative business, we were well cared for. He taught me the knowledge of the game. Perhaps, in a sense, I was trying to make up for my own part in playing the game, and now found the need to purge myself of my guilt.

I told him of the up-and-coming players and how they were more ruthless, didn't hold the same values as the old school hustlers, hopefully passing along my concern for his safety, as well as those with whom he had contact. I wanted to know, I needed to know, I had to know, if he truly endorsed what he had been doing and encouraged others to do.

From time to time, I would pause to see if he had anything to say, but he allowed me to speak uninterrupted. His silence rang in my ears louder than my own thoughts, and, when I was through, my father shared with me another lesson.

He had patiently listened to me make my argument until I ran out of words and became silent when looking into his dark eyes. He then proceeded to share his wisdom with me. The room was still and dark. The only light came from another room down the hall as his deep voice cut through the night and shattered my arguments.

"I don't blame the man for slinging the rock. You can't expect a man to flip burgers all day long. How else is he supposed to make it? You gotta make your own way." He proceeded to share with me how each man is responsible for his own future, his own destiny, and has to make his own mark and way on his own terms. He told me, in no uncertain terms, that people must provide for themselves and never rely on anyone to provide anything. To do so would ensure a quick downfall from which a person may or may not recover. He believed that for people to place themselves in the hands of another is a sign of weakness, and that to be dependent upon another is a denial of self-sufficiency. He talked for what seemed like an hour, though it was only a few minutes, and as he stood up to leave me to my thoughts, his backward glance told me that I was expected to live by his words.

As a child, we are dependent upon our caregivers, our guardians, our parents, or those responsible for our well-being, until we are taught or are forced to take care of ourselves.

It is when we are able to fend for ourselves that we grasp an independence to make our own decisions, to be our own person, and to find our way through life. My father was the provider and keeper of our home. I depended on him for love, guidance, money, and protection.

His occupation, being the keeper of crack, along with this lesson shared, told me that I was expected to always be responsible for making my own way. He shared the knowledge of his drug business with me, in order to ensure that I would be a self-sufficient person, not having to rely on anything or anyone to provide for me. To do so would be considered a sin. A mistake that would assure a swift downfall. For years, I lived by this lesson.

Yet, it is my Father who has taught me that I can rely on Him. I can trust Him to provide for me, knowing that He will give me what I need in this life in order to make it day by day, minute by minute, and second by second. It is my Father who promised that He would supply all of my needs, and it is His supply that will outlast and go beyond anything I could find in a toy store, purchase on a corner, inhale, snort, or inject, for His supply reaches the very depths of my soul and will carry me to eternity with Him. It is because of my Father that I will never have to worry, for I know that He knows what I stand in need of. He prepares me for my blessings, and He knows when I'm ready to receive that blessing.

Even when I, with my feeble attempts, resort to trying to make it on my own, to figure things out for myself, as I do so, He stands there, patiently waiting for me, with open arms, sometimes having to bless me in the midst of the mess I've created. For He knows that I, a mere human with all of my shortcomings, idiosyncrasies, and issues, could never find the peace that only He can give. I can't find my own way, much less make my way to the joy that He instills in those who are His.

He alone supplies the balm to heal broken hearts and broken lives, and even has the power to restore failing health. With each day that He gives, I realize that I could never make my own way. It's David's words in Psalm 119:105 that assure me during my journey:

> Thy word is a lamp unto my feet, and a light unto my path.

He knows that without His guidance, I am simply feeling my way through utter darkness, unsure of the pitfalls, potholes, snares, and traps that may befall me. In knowing this, He leads me, He guides me, He directs me, and He protects me.

My Father shows me His patience by holding me securely in the palm of His hand. More than that, He held me and kept me before I was even aware that I needed keeping. His hand protected me from seen and unseen danger. He shielded me from destruction, chastised me with instruction, and lifted me for His glorification. David tells us that His right hand upholds us. With each step, those taken and those yet-to-come, I know that He holds me yesterday, today, and tomorrow.

Like everyone else, I could ask why didn't He bring me into the knowledge of Him sooner? Why did it take so long for me to find His love? Yet, who am I to ask such questions? Who am I to expect Him to fall in line with my demands? He's God.

In asking those questions, my answers were found in the recorded lives of those found in His Word. For if Abraham had not left his family as instructed, if he had not had his Egypt experience where he lied to Pharaoh in order to protect himself, if he had not tried to listen to his wife in sleeping with Hagar the handmaiden, along with all of his other various experiences, then when confronted with sacrificing his son Isaac, he would not have been able to voice, with conviction, that the great El Shaddai will provide.

If David, my favorite Bible character, had not had his Goliath experience, his family drama where one son raped a daughter and another son campaigned against him for the throne, even his rooftop experience where he ultimately committed adultery, and had not been the shepherd boy, he would not have been able to eloquently write Psalm 23 saying "The Lord is my Shepherd."

My Father has allowed me to experience what I have experienced with all of its pain, its drama, life's consequences, and wounds, so that today I can boldly proclaim that He is good. He is faithful even when I am not; He is my sustainer, my provider, my maintainer, my joy, my peace, and the lover of my soul. So I trust in Him, my Father, who can make a way out of no way for me, as I watch Him open doors that man has shut. I see His direction where road maps cannot travel, and I trust His timing in the midst of turbulence as He holds me closer evermore. Today, I am able to voice with assuredness, the words written by the apostle Paul in Philippians 4:19:

> But my God shall supply all your need according to his riches in glory by Christ Jesus.

It is in His provision that I am blessed beyond measure, as He continuously transforms me with each day that He gives, into a new creature. Old things are passed away; behold, all things have become new.

LESSON SEVEN
You Can't Believe Everything You Hear

Though my immediate family is relatively small, I come from a tribe that consists of aunts, uncles, cousins, etc. I have a brood of uncles who range in age from close to my own to decades older. During my childhood, my father would not recognize his out-of-wedlock children. So, my uncles became my big brothers and looked out for me. One, two or three of them lived with us at one time or another. They took care of me. Whenever they came around, for a friendly visit or just to lay their heads down, I was excited and happy to see them. And though these were my mother's brothers, my father counted them as his own.

To me, they were the most handsome, funny, and coolest brothers in the city. They walked with a swagger and confidence that went above and beyond any of our neighborhood guys, and even though they weren't from our hood, their reputation preceded them.

They were tough guys, street fighters, and shoot-first-ask-questions-later kind of guys. On many occasions, we received word that one, two, or all of them had been in a rumble of sorts and left their opponents running with their tails tucked between their legs. I grinned with pride at the news. It was all about reputation and respect.

However, to them, some of their battles weren't worth it. Like the time one of my favorite uncles, while walking from the trolley to our home came upon a man who was severely beating his wife, girlfriend, or lover in the middle of the street. Despite his hard core, my uncle knew this was wrong and quickly jumped on and beat the man until he fell to the ground, only to then be attacked by the woman who received the initial beating, wielding a broom in her hand. Once he arrived at our home and told us what happened, he felt like a fool for defending the honor of a woman who didn't even realize she needed to be defended. It was this act of chivalry, along with "swag," street sense, and confidence that caused the women to swoon over my uncles.

The women who rarely gave me a backwards glance most days were overly nice when my uncles came around and readily parted their lips to give syrupy, sweet hellos, in an effort to later part their legs for my uncles.

My uncles didn't care anything about those girls, or any particular girl from what I could see. I knew this for sure because in the privacy of our home, they would talk about these women as if they were trash, voicing how easily they gave it up or were willing to do whatever was required to be called their girl—which was something I knew I'd never do.

I had my little boyfriends, and was even caught kissing the used-to-be cute boy who lived across the street in the back seat of our car while our mothers drove to a prayer meeting at the young and tender age of five. But, as I grew older, my father drilled into me that if I ever came up pregnant, he would kill me. I believed him. So, a few soft kisses were as far as I was ever willing to go with a guy. I never once gave another thought to what would happen to the boy who impregnated me; the fact that I'd be dead caused me to quickly dismiss him and the act of going too far with any boy from my mind.

Since most of my uncles either didn't know or have a relationship with their sperm donor of a dad, they looked to my father as his replacement.

Due to my grandmother's infidelities, my uncles' African-American heritage was mixed with races that ranged from Italian to

Puerto-Rican to the blood of my Asian grandfather. Of course, it never mattered to me who my grandmother chose to share her bed with; that was her business. The way I saw it, family was family.

When my uncles came around, we ran errands for my father and mother which took us to different areas of our hood and our city. It didn't matter where we were going—walking or riding—just being by their side or in their company gave me a sense of pride.

They were my uncles, my big brothers, and the men I looked to for guidance or a heads- up on a particular situation. Or, sometimes, I just had a day full of fun with them. Many of them worked on construction sites with my father and also went on to work with his other businesses. Whenever they came around, I looked forward to it—except the day one of them decided to act in such a way that my father was encouraged to teach yet another lesson.

It was a hot summer day. As usual, I was outside, playing with my friends and the game of the hour was double-dutch. In this game, two girls hold opposite ends of wire ropes covered in plastic. People sometimes use this type of rope to hang out laundry. However, the double-dutch rope is not to be confused with another type of laundry rope, because some ropes are not good for playing double-dutch.

The girls holding the opposite ends of the ropes twirl their arms in circles, the left arm turning clockwise while the right arm turns counter-clockwise, causing the ropes to smack the ground in a timely rhythm, one after the other. The players take turns jumping in between the ropes, and the trick is to jump in the center of the twirling rope, and to keep on jumping. To do this requires skill. If players jump in at the wrong time or are unable to keep jumping in conjunction with the timing of the rope, they're sure to receive a stinging rope smack or get tangled, both of which will bring about the end of their turn at jumping rope.

Should players make it in between the twirling ropes successfully, the rope twirlers and anyone standing by waiting for their turn chant the song of numbers that begins at 1 and goes as high as players are able, to keep on jumping. The challenge is that each set of ten requires a different acrobatic skill. "Tens" called for footsies, where feet had to go from their standing-still-running motion to hitting the ground at the same time. "Twenties" called for players to jump up and down like a pogo stick. In the "Thirties," players had to go around in a circle; "Forties" asked players to hop on one leg; "Fifties" required that players criss-crossed their feet, while "Sixties," "Seventies," "Eighties," and "Nineties" repeated what was already done. If players were lucky enough to reach one hundred, the rope turned faster and faster, and their feet had to keep up until "Smack!" Players were popped in the arms, legs, or, unfortunately, the faces by the stinging rope that had generated enough speed to bring about a red whelp on immediate impact.

I was good—sometimes good enough to reach one hundred—but, I was never an accomplished speed jumper and refused to even risk being popped to whelp status. So, I'd often stop jumping before the rope twirlers were able to get their speed up.

Double-dutch is something that you could play for hours and hours, and the very best double-dutch jumpers were found in my city. People learned to do tricks, cartwheels, and even entered competitions. But, for us, it was just another way to have fun. It was never that serious, just a means to an end—summer fun.

On this particular day, I was waiting for my turn to jump in, silently keeping the timing and rhythm of the twirling ropes in my head, in order to jump in at just the right time, when one of my uncles ran around the corner and down the street. He reminded me of Pig-Pen, that kid in the Charlie Brown cartoon with a cloud of dust around him whenever he took a step, due to the layer of dirt covering his body. This particular uncle had been working with my father that day on a construction site, so his jeans, white T-shirt, construction boots, and even his Afro were covered in a gray layer of dust.

I wondered why he was running and wondered more about the whereabouts of my father, so I decided to skip my turn, told my friends I'd be back, and met him at the bottom of our steps.

His eyes were frantic when he asked if my mother was in the house. I nodded my head and watched him leap up the steps, pull open the white storm door, and enter through the open front door. I didn't even give the storm door time to close behind him before I followed on his dusty heels.

He dropped his tool belt onto the porch floor and bellowed over and over again for my mother, impatiently waiting for her to respond. My mother, hearing the urgency in his voice, came out of the kitchen and looked into the face of my terrorized uncle.

"He's hurt. He got hurt on the job," my uncle said.

Of course, we understood "he" meant my father, and I could feel my heart begin to beat faster and faster.

"The dogs attacked him," he went on.

By this time, my mother was on the verge of hysteria, as she tried to grasp the words that came from her brother's lips. All she could get out of her mouth were sounds, not words,

"Wha? Wh? Wh!?!"

In an effort to calm her, my uncle grabbed her arms and told her, "We were about to leave the site, and this pack of wild dogs came up and attacked us. We tried to make it to the truck, but they jumped on him. They tore his clothes; they're all shredded. He's hurt bad."

My mother asked, "Where is he?"

"He's on his way," my uncle responded. "I got here first to tell you what happened. You might want to run him a hot bath and get the alcohol and bandages. He's gonna need it."

My mother never said another word; she simply went into her mode. She ran up the steps, and I could hear the water running. She ran down the steps, asking if he had arrived yet. Without waiting for an answer, she ran to the front door and poked her head out to see if my father was coming.

I stood there in the middle of the floor, wondering what I was supposed to do, if anything, while my uncle plopped down on the couch and a cloud of dust floated to the ceiling. He kept urging my mother to make sure she did this and did that to ensure my father's comfort upon his arrival, and my mother readily obeyed, all the while wringing her hands. I sat in the chair, not wanting to get mixed up with the dust that seemed to drift out of my uncle's pores and waited for my father to arrive home, bloodied, scratched, and torn to shreds.

It seemed like an hour passed until finally, I heard the door open and the heavy sound of my father's boots trekking across the porch floor. My mother ran to him with tear-filled eyes, preparing for the sight in front of her. She practically tackled him, placing her hands on his face, not even taking notice of his appearance.

"Are you alright? Here, let me help you!"she shouted. I'd never seen her show such emotion where he was concerned. When I saw my father, I wondered what all the fuss was about. But, it wasn't until my mother heard her brother's roaring laughter and turned to see him rolling around on the living room floor, dust and all, that she realized she'd been had.

My father pushed her away and asked what all of the nonsense was about, while my mother ran down for him the account given to her of the dog attack. It was then that my father taught yet another lesson with his response, "Don't believe everything you hear."

This humorous uncle, the jokester, had done it again. He

often looked for opportunities to trick his older sister when she was alone. She was always the focus of his jokes, and, like Lucy pulling the football away from Charlie Brown, she fell for them every time.

When my younger brother was being potty-trained, my uncle actually went out and purchased a fake replica of stool and threw it on the floor. My mother went to the trouble of getting a bucket of water and cleaning supplies, all the while sucking her teeth and fussing about cleaning up her son's mess. When she knelt down on the carpet to clean up "the mess," my uncle whooped and hollered. She'd been had again.

He had tricked us many times, but it was this escapade that really brought my father's lesson home. My uncle had found great joy and delight in tricking his sister that day, though she didn't share his sentiment. My father thought all of us were silly and quickly dismissed what looked like a three-ring circus, with my uncle being the ringleader. Still, the lesson "Don't believe everything you hear" was voiced and well-received.

In today's society, there are many avenues to get the latest gossip and hear the latest rumors. Many tabloid magazines plaster what they've heard or deem to be true without investigating the source, ruining lives and families.

Even worse, many people take great delight in hearing of the misfortunes of others—true or not—in an effort to make themselves feel better and soothe their insecurities.

I remember playing the game "Whisper Down the Line" where the first person in line came up with a simple sentence or a tongue-twisting string of words, whispered it in the ear of the next person one time, and so on, until it reached the last person in line. Usually, during the course of the message being passed from one person to another, the participants' faces screwed up because they weren't sure if what they heard was correct. So, they modified the inaudible consonants and vowels by either adding or taking away from them, and then passed on what they thought they heard to the next person. By the time the message reached the last person, it was never the same as the beginning message, adding more credence to the lesson that you can't believe everything that you hear. The sentence could be something as simple as "It's a sunny day," but by the time it reached the last person in line, it was misconstrued into "Pooky got shot trying to steal a Popsicle from the corner store."

It was this lesson that encouraged me to always check out the source of something. If someone said it, I refused to take it for the gospel truth without some sort of investigation. Even if they had a backup source, unless I spoke with that person, it wasn't credible.

Truth is as sincere as the deliverer, and often it's the credibility of the deliverer that determines the acceptance of what has been said. For example, knowing that my uncle was a jokester and a prankster who liked to bend and twist the truth simply to gauge the reaction of others or to get a good laugh, his words could not be taken seriously as truth. It was impossible to know when he was being honest and when he was not. It is the same as the boy who cried wolf. After so many times of falsely crying wolf, when the wolf did make an appearance, no one believed the boy, causing dire consequences.

This lesson taught me to be ever so skeptical. To listen twice and to think about what I'd heard three times as much. It taught me to view everyone with a hidden agenda or as if they were trying to pull the wool over my eyes in an effort to showcase me as a fool. These words caused me only to believe what I saw with my own eyes and felt with my own touch. It was this lesson that, again, solidified my distrust for people. After all, if my uncle tricked his sister and enjoyed it, then what would those outside my family do to get their jollies?

When I heard the gospel of Jesus Christ, His death, burial, and resurrection, my father's lesson was challenged. He taught me to trust my instincts and no one else's. If I didn't hear it, it wasn't true. If I didn't see it, it never happened. If I couldn't touch it, it wasn't real. If I couldn't smell it, it never existed. If I was unable to taste it, it had to be fake.

My Father claimed to love me, yet I could not see Him, hear Him speak, reach out to touch Him, smell His scent, or taste Him. From the lesson my father taught, my five senses could not line up with what the Bible said. But, instead of turning away from it, I wanted to learn more about this God and what He had to offer.

I learned that He spoke to me through the Bible, the written and inspired Word of God, and that if He said it, it was going to come to pass. He even knew me before my existence. I realized His scent is found in the rain He allows to fall, the faint and delicate scent in a flower, and all He has created. His Word is the food I can taste. I must not only read it, but digest it or meditate on it every day, in order to live a life pleasing to Him. It supplies the necessary nutrients for my spiritual growth. I believe He can and continues to see me. If I meditate on His Word, I can see Him for who He truly is—my Father who loved me before I knew Him and continues to do so.

It's in coming to know my Father that I understand faith—my ability to believe what my senses cannot fathom based on what He has told me. It's my faith that enables me to trust His guidance, to rely on His direction in my life, and to stand on His promises for all He has told me in His Word is true.

Noah commenced to build an ark based on his faith in the Creator who told him it was going to rain. Even though Noah had no clue what rain was, he continued to construct the ark. I must have that same faith.

Abraham was told to leave his family and venture towards a land he could not see, perhaps never even heard of. He had to rely on the promise he was given—that he would be father of many nations. I must have that same faith.

It was by faith that Moses was able to lead God's people out of bondage, through the Red Sea, and to march around the city of Jericho every day in order for the walls to come down.

These examples tell me that I must follow where He leads. The walls I've erected in my life, based on my fears, insecurities, and five senses, will come down if I simply have faith in Him, my Father who knows me better than I could ever know myself. If I trust Him as a child trusts her father, if I have faith in what He has told me in His Word, then my life will be blessed, as well as those that I encounter.

There may be days when I have questions about His plans for my life or the course that I travel, but I must concur and live by the lyrics in "Victory" by Brenda Waters:

> I don't know how, how He's going to do it.
> He didn't tell me when, when He's going to fix it.
> But I know, He's gonna make a way for me.
> He's gonna give me the victory.

The Hebrew writer gives the definition of faith in Hebrews 11:1:

> Now faith is the substance of things hoped for, the evidence of things not seen.

Having faith in God calls for me to trust Him beyond the shadow of any and every doubt, without fear, hesitation, explanation, or justification. It's taking my Father, my God, at His Word in realizing that He knows what's best for me. Should I have questions, doubts, or fears; despair; or be in need of comfort or strength, all He wants me to know is in His Word. I need not seek out a soothsayer, cling to a rabbit's foot, roll a dice, rub a crystal ball, or search out a psychic. He alone is truth. As I live this life longing to please Him, I rest in the totality that "God said it, I believe it, and that settles it."

LESSON EIGHT
Never Love Anyone More Than Me

I had my first boyfriend, or at least that's what I called him, when I was five years old. He was the same age as me and lived across the street. He and his brothers would come over to our house every day after school until one of his parents arrived home. To us, the confirmation of a childlike romance meant nothing more than sharing some penny candy and being able to actually say we were boyfriend and girlfriend.

This is the same young man I was caught kissing on the floorboards of the back seat, while our mothers drove to prayer meeting. Other than that, we were merely friends who lived across the street from each other and considered each other cute.

I later learned that by hood standards, most neighborhood relationships lasted barely more than two weeks before there was a new flavor of the month or the soon-to-be-kicked-to-the-curb companion felt the same. Most relationships, by kid standards, were never really serious, and even when we "broke up," we were still friends. There weren't any hard feelings. Those hard feelings were only felt by the teenagers and adults whose emotions and hormones were caught up in the crossfire of love.

Other than my young five-year-old kissing bandit of a boyfriend, I never officially dated any of the other guys in our neighborhood. Instead, we were friends, playing basketball, riding bikes, sharing penny candy, and even looking out for each other.

Although I never spoke of my two-week childlike love for anyone, I did become rather infatuated with one of the older boys in our hood. To be quite honest, it wasn't his physical appearance I was attracted to. It was his stroll, cockiness, and self-assuredness that reeled me in, causing me to honor him with the title Swagger.

Whenever he walked up and down the street, Swagger's shoulders were straight and his chest was poked out, like he knew he was going somewhere. Even if he was going only to the corner store, I eagerly watched his stroll, ready to follow.

Swagger would kick it with his crew, playing basketball with them, hanging on the corner, and probably doing what brothas barely on the brink of manhood do. He was actually the older brother of one of my girlfriends and was at least five years older than me.

I never mentioned my secret crush for Swagger to anyone until my father and I went for ice cream one night. That was the summer night when I was taught yet another lesson, after the sun had gone down, but humidity lingered in the hood.

It was so hot; some folk felt so sticky they would take more than one bath a day, not only to get rid of the summer funk, but also to cool off. It seemed like people couldn't find relief from the heat anywhere, unless they were fortunate enough to have an air conditioner. Even then, most homes only had them in one room. They were the kind that sat perched in the window, so people had to choose which room to cool off and that's the room where everyone congregated.

We kept our air conditioner in the dining room window. I'm not sure why, maybe because it was in the back of the house and would require a lot of effort for someone to steal or because it countered any heat generated from the small kitchen next to the dining room.

Regardless, the summer hood heat caused people to

search out ways to cool off. No one had a pool, for the homes weren't made for such things. The back yard of our row homes was nothing more than a small, fenced-in block of cement where weeds struggled to grow through the cracks. Even if parents bought one of those plastic round pools, they didn't usually stay around long. Too many kids tried to pile in and broke it or someone stole it. We didn't have a pool and neither did any of my friends. There was always the option of walking over to the public pool at the neighborhood recreation center, but it wasn't worth the walk, and I also heard that the "trifling" sort peed in that pool.

To beat the heat, some would illegally turn on the fire hydrant. Kids could run around in the water either fully clothed, partially clothed, or unclothed, as the powerful stream of water from the hydrant's mouth hit them full-force.

I never liked playing in the hydrant much and was always sure to keep my distance, just in case one of the guys thought it would be funny to grab me and carry me directly into the stream of water, like they had done to so many other girls. Some of the older kids would press their butts against the mouth of the hydrant, causing the water to take on a geyser effect, as it arced into the air, so that cars or kids could run underneath without getting wet.

The use of the fire hydrant was one of the quickest ways to beat the summer heat, but it was always short-lived because of the policemen who came around and shut the fire hydrant off, daring any of the water-soaked kids to turn it back on. It didn't matter that having it on affected the water pressure in the neighborhood. Who cares about water pressure when the heat is beating down on your head? Still, when shut off, sometimes it was turned back on time and time again, and sometimes it wasn't. It depended on how hot it was and who was bold enough to defy the law of the land, which was usually overruled by hood laws anyway. Since I never ventured to dance and splash in the fire hydrant water, my friends and I would seek out other means to cool off.

Sometimes all it took was a sweet, yet tangy water ice. A concoction of shaved ice mixed with every flavor imaginable—piña colada, cherry, blueberry, lemon, bubble gum, mango, orange, or even a combination of all of them. Whatever flavor we chose was painted on our tongue and lips as we smacked the tasty, cold treat, trying to make it last for as long as possible.

It was either water ice or the ice cream truck playing monotonous droning music, alerting every child of its approach. We usually chose water ice because it gave us the chance to venture a few blocks over to buy our treats.

However, my mother rarely wanted water ice or something from the ice cream truck. She'd rather have her frozen treat from the ice cream parlor because it sold more than the basic napoleon flavors of vanilla, chocolate, and strawberry. The ice cream parlor not only sold different flavors, it even sold frozen yogurt, sherbet, various kinds of candy, sodas, chips, and hot dogs, making it more like a corner store than an ice cream parlor.

Its location was more than a mile from our home, which meant we couldn't walk; we'd have to drive over there. I didn't mind the drive and neither did my father, but on this day my mother didn't want to go. She asked us to get ice cream for her. Although I'd rather spend time with friends than have to share space with my father, whose personality could change faster than a chameleon's color, I never turned down an opportunity to go anywhere. And so, we went, my father and I, just the two of us, after the sun had gone down, to get the ice cream that couldn't be purchased on any ice cream truck.

My father's favorite flavor was coffee ice cream, so it was a good deal for him to go there. I didn't dabble in what I considered to be exotic flavors. Chocolate or vanilla was the extent of my palette; I just wanted to go for the ride.

On a hot summer night like this one, the ice cream parlor was surprisingly empty. Like most businesses in the hood, it occupied a one-step, small, storefront building with a huge, gated window in the front and one entrance. The door had a bell attached to the top, so when we entered, the owner was aware of our presence.

It wasn't like one of the ice cream parlors that you saw on television where kids would gather to listen to the juke-box, or the employees wore starched, white shirts and crisp, white hats. There weren't any soda machines or decorative canisters. Our ice cream store was a narrow room that held two white, glass-encased coolers that held at least sixteen containers of ice cream for the customers to gaze at. There was one round table with two chairs in the back of the room, but I never saw anyone sitting there. Music blared from an old radio on the shelf behind the counter, out of customers' reach. It was dimly lit, and I always looked for the source of the eerie, yellow glow that seemed to dominate the room. It was a soft glow, but strange nonetheless. There were a few boxes holding candy bars and chips perched alongside bottles of soda and a small grill for hot dogs. That was pretty much it. But, no one really cared that this store didn't resemble the iconic ice cream parlor; we simply wanted the treats we could not get from the ice cream truck.

At 11 years old, I was tall enough to peer into the glass-encased ice cream freezer. It seemed to hold bottomless, round containers of ice cream in flavors such as black raspberry, coffee, pistachio, butter pecan, rainbow sherbet, and a few others I would never think to try.

We ordered our items from the woman behind the counter who rarely spoke or hardly acknowledged we were there. She never gave a friendly hello and didn't even ask what flavor we wanted. We simply told her our desires, and she commenced to digging into the ice cream, making the crater that had been formed bigger and deeper. She handed us the ice cream cone or cup in silence and didn't part her lips until it was time for us to pay for our items by telling us the amount of purchase. That was it, pretty cut and dried. No "have a nice day," or "hope to see you again." Nah, this was the hood, no time for meaningless talk. She could care less if we came back to patronize her business. Or, if she did, she sure didn't show it. We silently took our order without a "thank you" and walked back to the car.

I was enjoying my frozen treat, a scoop of chocolate ice cream perched on top of a sugar cone, when my friend's older brother, Swagger, walked toward me. I could tell it was him by his stroll, before I even looked into his face. I'm sure the silly little grin I had, painted with chocolate ice cream, must have been quite a sight, but who cared, my ghetto basketball knight was walking towards us. Although I was sure he never noticed me before, there was no way he wouldn't see me this day because I stood directly in his pathway. And he did see me, for he actually spoke with a nonchalant "hey," and at that moment, I promise you, time stood still.

My senses were on overload, not from the stifling summer heat which seemed to disappear, but from the warmth of his smile, or at least the smile I told myself I saw. I couldn't even feel the ice cream dripping down my hand. All I could hear was his voice. I don't even know if I responded to his greeting because my heartbeat drowned out any sounds. It even drowned out my father's voice because I didn't hear his angry words or see him standing directly in front of me with disgust on his face, until the love fog lifted from my eyes.

My father's eyes shone with anger and his lips were twisted into a grimace I thought I understood, but didn't. I thought he was upset because with every drip of my ice cream, I was wasting his money. He sneered at me, "Get in the car!" and gave a slight shove to emphasize his point. I obeyed and began to lick up as much of the quickly melting ice cream as possible, so as not to make a mess in his immaculate black car and also hopefully to extinguish his anger. As I glanced around, my knight in shining armor had disappeared. Wherever he was going, he'd departed quickly and was nowhere to be seen.

My father came around to the driver's side, jumped in, placed my mother's package of ice cream between us, and started his car. Before speaking, I glanced over at him, hoping to ease the tension. I didn't want him to think that I didn't appreciate my ice cream treat. But, in an effort to take the attention off my treat and to lighten his mood as well as my own, my words spoke of my basketball prince. I asked if he had seen him, the guy that lives around the corner, my friend's older brother. I told him how well he played basketball, and how I thought he was such a great guy. I even accidently told him how much I liked him. I must've talked for what seemed like forever, all the while taking short licks on my ice cream.

Had I been paying attention, I would've realized that my father's silence did not indicate approval. His anger was escalating.

He stopped me in mid-sentence with words that sounded as if they'd come from somewhere deep within his gut, giving them a low and menacing feel, "I don't care who you think you like, don't you never let me see you act that way over any man again unless it's me. Don't you never love no one more than me."

I was stunned into silence. That's what this was all about? He had seen and heard my admiration and confession of a childlike crush on an innocent teenage boy who barely knew that I existed, and it somehow threatened him. It had absolutely nothing to do with the melting of the ice cream or even the mess I had made, making my hand all sticky.

It wasn't even about the possible mess I could've made in his precious car. He was jealous over my public display of a never-to-blossom love that was directed at someone other than himself.

I'm sure that the look on my face displayed my shock, but he never even glanced over at me, never said another word as we drove home. The only sound I heard was the wind whistling through the open window.

The ice cream lost its flavor. I continued to eat in order to prevent it from dripping on me and in the car. But, it was as if my tongue couldn't even taste the chocolate anymore. The taste buds didn't recognize what they were eating. They were shocked by what I heard. As a matter of fact, all five of my senses were in shock. Not only could I no longer taste what I was eating, but also the city sounds were drowned out by his words echoing in my brain. If the ice cream was dripping down my hand, I couldn't feel it. My watery eyes held back tears that were on the brink of spilling over, but had been taught to remain unfallen. The summer heat didn't even have an effect on me anymore. I was numb.

I never expected that my father, whom I adored and I believed adored me, could feel threatened by the natural instinct of a supposed love for another boy or man. To him, I was his baby girl, the one thing he did right, who loved him unconditionally. He did not want that love for him, even if it was childlike and dwelled within the realm of a father-daughter bond, to be broken or challenged. He was responding like a jealous lover, a green-eyed controlling boyfriend. That was my father's take on my confession of love, adolescent crush or not. He felt as if something was, or could be on the verge of, being taken away from him. So, he became territorial, almost like a pit bull marking his plot of ground. I was stunned.

From then on, I was always careful to live in accordance with the lesson I learned that summer night, secretly keeping any resemblance of like or hopeful love for future boyfriends harbored in my heart. Even if my liking them turned into an innocent crush or a budding romance, I would never allow my true feelings to be known. Even when I went on dates— that my father knew of—I was sure to speak of the courter in a nonchalant way, so as to live within the bounds of my father's lesson. When I thought he had perhaps outgrown his lesson or changed his mind towards it, I was quickly reminded of his jealousy when he forbid me to see someone he thought I had too many feelings for. As long as I remembered the lesson, I could date, dance, and court any guy he approved of. I could've lied to myself that my father was simply overprotective and looked upon his actions as a way of wanting what was best for me, but that was furthest from the truth. He wanted and needed to be first and foremost in my life, for as long as he was able to control it.

How contradictory this lesson is to the love we must have towards our Father. It was the once-upon-a-time tax collector and disciple of Christ who recorded the words of our Savior in Matthew 10:37:

> He that loveth father or mother more than me is not worthy of me: and he that loveth son or daughter more than me is not worthy of me.

It is the Creator who loved me before I was a thought in any human mind and who continues to love me, in spite of myself. When I look at all He gave for me—His life—so I could have the opportunity of a better life in Him, it causes me to realize and live by His lessons on love. To love Him more than anyone, love myself because He created me, love others, and even love my enemies. If my declarations and actions of love were based solely on me and the encounters I've had with others, then my love would be limited and carry with it stipulations no one could measure up to.

From my Father, I have learned to love unconditionally, for only God could love me just as I am, not jumping through hoops, but simply to be me—the woman He created to obey His Word and to love Him for the God that He is. Only He could demonstrate true love and the deepness of love, enabling me to do the same with friends, family, husband, children, and even those who are looking for love, its meaning, and how to love and be loved.

It's a love that does not judge and is able to forgive, even without receiving an apology. A love that helps those in need and can do so when a request hasn't been made. A love that touches, feels, and protects the heart. A love that is respectful of the differences in all of us, not condemning, but appreciating, learning, and embracing them.

The love of God enables me to see others as my Father sees them, not as I would. For my eyes are clouded, my vision is limited, and sometimes what I see may not be the way things really are. When I'm able to see others as He sees them—people who are loved by the same God, a God who reaches out to them and cares for them just as much as He cares for me, and wants what's best for all—then I am truly embracing the true meaning of His love.

For me, to know Him is to love Him. As His child, I am required to live as He commands and put Him first and foremost in my life. My love for my Father is to exceed any love that I have for my husband, my children, my parents, siblings, and friends. This is not a hardship if I allow myself to open my heart, soul, and spirit, and get to know Him, for He already knows me. With every breath He gives, with every step I'm allowed to take, I worship, praise, and love Him, realizing I am because He is.

This love does not excuse wrongdoing, nor offer a pass where He has drawn the line, but it strives to help others to understand that He wants what's best for us, in accordance with His Word, because of the love He has for us.

One of the very first Bible verses I memorized as a child continues to speak to me today:

For God so loved the world, that He gave His only be-gotten Son; that whosoever believeth in Him should not perish, but have everlasting life. (John 3:16)

Yes, I am able to love Him because He first loved me. I can only experience this love from the one who defines love, my Father, in whom I breathe, live, and have my very being.

LESSON NINE
Do Unto Others...Then Split

It was never uncommon to see our family pile into our car to go to one of our favorite destinations—the beach in Wildwood, N. J. We, along with one or two of our neighbors and their families, would carpool the hour-and-a-half to two-hour drive with my father's shiny, black car leading the way, followed by our neighbors' station wagon, and other vehicles. Cars were full of parents, children, beach blankets, beach toys, changes of clothes, and coolers bursting with fried chicken, potato salad, sandwiches, chips, ice, drinks, and other snacks.

Of course, before heading out, mothers urged their children to use and reuse the bathroom, but even then, it seemed once we left the city limits with the sprawling highway before us, someone's bladder was always on the verge of springing a leak. So, the train of cars would pull over for a pit stop. Not at a rest stop, mind you. For some unknown reason, we never frequented public restrooms. Instead, the cars would line up, one behind the other, on the side of the highway, while mothers led their children to a grassy area far away from passersby. I was always on the lookout for creepy, crawly creatures and tried to pee as quickly as possible just to get it over with. I thought it was unfair that boys and men could simply unzip, undo, and unleash their stream, while girls and women had to unfasten, unzip, disrobe, squat, unleash without control of the stream, and handle their business as fast as possible with their bottoms exposed to the world, wildlife included.

Once safely back in the vehicles, car excursion games resumed, naps continued, and adults chatted about the goings on of the hood left behind. The further away we traveled from our city, the more the scenery changed. Gone were the asphalt streets, concrete pavements, smog-filled air, noisy buses, honking cars, clanging trolleys, barking dogs, and crowded streets. Ahead of us was a stretch of highway lined with grassy fields and tall trees. Those grassy fields gave way to farmland occupied by cows and horses. Those cows and horses were replaced by more fields and trees, and even the air had a different aroma. It could be my lungs were in a state of shock due to the freshness of the air, but my father told me what I considered fresh air was merely horse manure, yet I kept my face to the wind as it blew through my hair. It felt good to be able to be away from the city, headed for the ocean.

After riding for more than an hour, no matter how many games kids played, or songs we hummed along with on the radio, or roadside pit stops were made, children become rather antsy. No one was able to truly stretch their legs. After being side by side, no matter how much family members love each other, there comes a time when even the most patient and easygoing child or adult will begin to wonder and even ask, "Are we there yet?" or "How much farther?" until finally those questions are answered, not verbally, but by the aroma.

You could actually smell the soon-to-be-seen ocean in the air. It was almost like you could sense the salt in the water. The smell was not pleasant, but not as bad as the polluted air of the city. It was just different. Fresher, perhaps, and the more we drove, the faster our hearts beat and the antsier we became.

Our excitement was justified by the beach attire worn by those we passed as we drew closer to the shores. Gone were the jeans and sneakers worn by most in our neighborhood.

These people wanted their skin to have direct contact with the sun, so it could be sun-kissed. Men and boys wore bathing trunks which stopped right above their knees or the daring Adonises chose to boast of their manhood with a tightly fitted Speedo®, while they walked around poking out their bare chests, showing off the countless hours spent lifting weights. However, there were even those men who obviously hadn't touched a weight of any sort in quite some time, unless the beer bottles they lifted over their beer guts to their lips counted.

Women and girls wore one-piece or bikini bathing suits, depending on their age or willingness to bare it all. However, regardless of gender, there were some scantily clad and others whose flesh practically screamed to be released from the colorful Spandex. Brightly colored beach towels were draped across shoulders, tucked under arms, or dragged behind, as feet smacked flip-flops or shoeless, tread lightly.

Our hearts beat faster and we couldn't wait for the drivers to find their parking spaces. Upon arrival, everyone peeled themselves from the car seats and while adults stretched their legs, children began to scamper and jump up and down eagerly wanting to race to the ocean that roared less than a mile away. Everyone carried something, and we looked like an army headed for a mission. Sometimes we had to walk for blocks just to make it to the boardwalk, which was nothing more than miles and miles of a wooden platform erected above the sand, lined with stores selling foods from every ethnic cuisine, arcades, tourist shops, and games and jutted out into piers that held amusement rides for all ages.

Across the boardwalk was one of the hottest foundations for feet to absorb—sand. Even the most anxious child had to stop and take note of the heat before removing shoes. The summer sun was so hot it caused wavy lines in the air over the burning sand.

The beach was a sight to behold. Adults sashayed along the

sand, children ran around covered in sand from head to toe, grandparents sat under umbrellas jabbed in the sand, and the daring ventured into the ocean ahead.

This was the original tanning bed. Men and women would coat themselves with tanning oil, hoping to darken the pigmentation of their skin, no matter how hot it was or how long it took. I'd seen some turn a painful beet-red, as they burned themselves for a tan that only lasted a few weeks, but damaged their skin for a lifetime. Of course, children at the beach never gave this a second thought. All we wanted was to splash in the water, collect beautiful seashells, poke at the jellyfish that lay exposed on the sand, build sandcastles, or dig as if we were trying to find China. While we played, we tanned naturally.

Seagulls were flying low, waves were high, and the sun was beaming as we trekked our way to wherever our parents decided to set up camp. After finding an area large enough for all of us, we dumped our paraphernalia and began to pull and tug at our clothes, in order to bare our bodies for the world to see and the sun to burn. If we were hungry anymore, we didn't know it. If we were sleepy, we didn't show it. We were at the beach—the place to run wild and free, and actually make a mess in the sand without being yelled at. Still, before we could go, our parents emphasized the rules—Don't go too far out in the water and look out for one another.

We started to unpack our bags, and our mothers began to plot out their positions on the sand, so that the sun could beat down on their skin. Don't ever let anyone tell you that black people don't tan. The people I know rather enjoy it. Our skin has the ability to become darker as well, and I believe that we tan easier than any other race. I'm not sure where the myth came from that we don't tan, but it is an untruth.

It was during this time that my father taught me another lesson. He and the other men never enjoyed the beach. They'd rather go to the boardwalk, and we wouldn't see them again until it was time to leave. They would give their wives or girlfriends all of the money they needed for treats, rides, and games. But, the men separated themselves from us. I don't know if their actions were a manly type of thing. I just know it was the way things were done.

Before their departure, my father walked up to me and with his feet planted and his knees bent, and told me he had something for me. I wasn't sure what to think. Was this a ploy or a prize? I couldn't think of a reason for a gift. Though I'd been a good girl, not complaining about the ride or even mumbling about peeing in the grass, what reason did he have to present me with a gift? Or perhaps, it wasn't a gift as I supposed. With him, you never knew what to expect. From behind his back he produced a rolled-up towel he said he wanted me to have. He said he'd bought it for me because it held a truth. I was excited and began to unroll it, imagining lying on my own plot of sand after running through the ocean's waves.

When I unrolled the scrolled towel, I saw a cartoon character that looked like one of the characters from the story book "Where the Wild Things Are." It had brown skin, bushy hair, purple shorts, and flip-flops. He had a beach towel around his shoulders, a beach bucket in his hand, and a smirk on his face. Above his head in purple letters were the words "Do Unto Others…" and below his feet was the conclusion "…Then Split." I thought it was a cute towel— the cartoon character, that is—and, being taught to be grateful for what's given, I told my father thank you, with a smile.

He asked me to walk with him for a moment while he sent the other guys ahead towards the boardwalk. I tucked my towel under my little arm and grabbed his hand, as he picked me up in his massive arms so I wouldn't have to walk on the hot sand, which was thoughtful. But, I'd be expected to trek all the way back to our beach camp with quick steps, in order to keep my feet from being scorched by the grains of sand.

It was during our hike at the beach that he expounded on this lesson of "Do Unto Others…Then Split." He told me that it was important for us to do what we do and not allow people to get back at us. We should never allow anyone the opportunity to get the upper hand, dispense a payback, or execute revenge. If anyone was the executor, he was, and, therefore, he had to be in control of his present and future. He believed that once he made a decision to make a move, it wasn't his job to stay around and watch the fallout or even worry about the repercussions, because if his plans were executed correctly, he wouldn't have to worry about it. He lived by the creed that we should do what we've made up our minds to do and keep moving. There was no time for regrets; judgments should be pondered ahead of time; anything else was a waste of time. Whenever he talked, I allowed him to do so until he talked himself out, so I was silent as I looked into his dark eyes.

There is a stark reality between what I was taught and what I've come to know as truth. My father's words taught that we should not be sympathetic, have compassion, or be moved by the pain of another. His commandments preached thou shalt not love, thou shalt not feel, thou shalt not care. Yet, I did. I loved, cared, and felt compassion in my heart for my family and others. What I felt in my heart fought against what my father taught, causing me to hide and mask my caring feelings. I was expected to be rigid and cold, heartless and cruel. To him, it was how he'd been able to survive. And so, I learned to dress my heart with armor, in order to appear to be what he expected. But, on the inside, my heart was about to burst open, giving away my secret of being created to love just as my Father loves. I was created to have compassion, as opposed to a heart of ice, and to live by the Golden Rule or Matthew 7:12:

Do unto others, as you would have them do unto you.

My Father unselfishly gave of Himself in order to change the lives and destinies of men and women. His earthly ministry called for Him to meet the needs of those who were sick and hurting. With His touch, even the very contact of His garment, lives were made whole, sins were forgiven, love was restored, peace prevailed, and what was once considered damaged was renewed.

It's when I am willing to look at all He has done for me—and I could never do enough to deserve His blessings—that I realize I am required to treat people with the same regard as He's treated me, with love. Not based on who they are, the color of their skin, the amount of money they possess, where they live, the goals they might have set, or even their actions towards me, for He encourages me to "turn the other cheek" (Luke 6:29), "go the extra mile" (Matthew 4:11), and even "love my enemies" (Luke 6:27).

I have a lingering question about those who treat me wrong, seem to have it in for me, or find joy in my suffering and delight in my despair. As His child, am I required to continue to treat them as I want to be treated, or am I to forgo what He's told me and give them a taste of their own medicine? My human nature calls for me to dispense a payback. But again, He is my example, for while walking among men and women unselfishly giving of Himself, He was placed on trial for the crime of loving me. He was beaten beyond recognition and He refused to say a word. He was spit upon, yet He never raised His hand and said "Enough!" A crown of thorns was pressed into His head, and while the blood trickled down His face, He did not curse, mumble, or even complain. He was taunted, teased, pushed, and shoved as He carried a cross down a narrow road, and it was meant for me. He didn't have to go through it. He could've put a stop to the madness that led to Calvary. After all, He was and is God. He could've destroyed those who dispensed punishment without reason, but He didn't.

With every strike of the nails driven into His hands and feet while His body absorbed the pain, He silently suffered without protest. While hanging between yesterday and today, while His crucifiers laughed and snickered, He could've screamed, "Father, forgive them not!" but instead He looked on with love. He looked down the halls of time and could see me some 2,000 years later, trying to make it on my own. He could see me and others like me, living from day to day, week to week and year to year, holding on to His example. He looked up to His Father and my Father and simply said, "Father, forgive them, for they know not what they do." (Luke 23:34). If He could be so forgiving, who am I to refuse forgiveness?

It is also my brother Paul who gives the answer in Romans 12:19:

> Dearly beloved, avenge not yourselves, but rather give place unto wrath: for it is written,
> Vengeance is mine; I will repay, saith the Lord.

However, I don't allow folks to use me, abuse me, toss me around, and stand by with my hands in my pockets while slaps are dispensed or wrongdoing is directed towards me. For my Father also expects His children to be wise in our dealings; however, when a wrongdoing occurs, it's not my job to plot and scheme or make plans to be the dispenser of a lesson taught or a wrong righted. My Father, who sees all and knows all in the final scheme of things, will take care of me, as well as those who do not have my best interest at heart, and live as if it's their sole responsibility to bring hell to my doorstep. I am simply required to live as He would expect, for in wearing His name, belonging to Him, and abiding in Him, my life is not my own.

☨ LESSON TEN
She Ain't Care Enough To Stay

Marriage is hard work. I've heard people say in order for a relationship to be successful, each person has to give a fifty/fifty effort, but that's not true. Each person is required to give 100 percent and even more—if that's possible. Their all is necessary in order for it to work, and even then, it's not guaranteed. I've been married for quite some time, and I don't believe there's a handbook out there that can prepare you or your spouse for the unexpected twists and turns, the joys, and perhaps even the sorrows that come with being married. For with each day God gives, we are forever growing and changing. Being married calls for the groom and the bride to be able to adapt to the changes.

Perhaps God was exercising a sense of humor when He created men and women to be so different. Maybe He wanted to keep our lives interesting, for marriage takes work, commitment, and an unconditional love.

For years, I watched my parents live in an unhappy state. I only witnessed them kiss one time, and that was only done after constant urging and begging for a sign of affection, which meant the performance wasn't genuine. It was done more for the benefit of satisfying the request.

Given their history, I imagine a therapist would surmise it was a marriage doomed from the beginning. The odds were stacked against them. Odds that included a twenty-plus year age difference, my father being the older of the two. Odds such as his need to control and be secretive, not to mention his countless affairs. My mother's odds included her passive nature, contentment to be controlled, refusal to question for the sake of keeping peace, and acceptance of abuse. It made for interesting living. I believe she held on to the relationship just to be able to claim we were a family, as opposed to the imagined shame that would come from a "failed" marriage.

Abuse is usually identified as something of a physical nature—hits, smacks, slaps, punches, kicks, shoves, and pushes. However, as an adult, I realized abuse can also be mental and emotional, which harbors a deeper scar. A bruise will fade, a cut will mend and heal, but mental and emotional abuse renders inner scars that can fester and even resurface in an instant. Being placed in an environment where one is made to feel inferior or less than sufficient weighs on the mind and the spirit, and affects the body. Verbal abuse of screaming and degrading words spit from the lips of the abuser leave the abused feeling worthless, unloved, and uncared for. If the abuse includes both aspects, physical and verbal, the result is quite different. Because the abused, sometimes unknowingly, wears it as a medal, secretly congratulating themselves for hanging in there or sacrificing their happiness to make it work. Eventually, this "medal of honor" becomes an anchor and again, the abused individual may not even be aware of its transition. This type of abuse weighs the spirit down so gradually that the abused person may even become comfortable with the weight, or their minds are twisted into thinking this is the cross they were meant to bear.

They are drowning in a sea of degradation; the water has flooded their spirits and entombs their souls. Unfortunately, they are oblivious to the churning, frigid waters, unless their minds are freed from the entanglement of the anchor.

At home, as time progressed, every day it was like living inside a ticking time bomb on the verge of exploding. Because as people change, grow, mature, and come into their own, a realization comes forth, demanding that people welcome the change, adapt to and accept the change, or deny the change. However, this situation is magnified when one person is undergoing a metamorphosis, and the other seems to remain stagnant.

Such was the case with my mother. She had married at a young age and after years of accepting what was given, told, and ordered, the moment arrived when she had come into her own. She wanted to know what it felt like to be able to make her own money. She wanted to be one of the many career-minded women who were able to raise a family, take care of her home, and still have a nine-to-five job. She wanted to drive her own car, pay for her own gasoline, and even pump it by herself.

I don't believe she loved her family any less with her newfound desire and discovery. But, she did begin to love herself and realized what she could become, if she made the effort to step out and be her own woman.

My father, needless to say, didn't approve. After all, he made more than enough money to provide for ten or more families—even if it was by illegal means. More importantly, it was a threat to his control. I understand how in living in a society that downgrades the worth of an African-American man, that man's home, of all places, is where he needs to feel not only love, but respect, support, and possibly, the need to be in control.

Yet, progress won't be stopped. It might be hindered or slowed down, but eventually, progress is going to take its rightful place. It's also difficult to discourage a determined woman who has her mind focused and set on something.

Such was the case with my mother. She studied the drivers' manual and obtained her drivers' license. In the morning, she hurried through her domestic duties, always keeping her home tidy and neat, but once complete, her daytime hours were spent less watching soap operas and more focusing on the classified section of the daily newspaper. She enrolled in night classes at a local school and was on the road to betterment.

My father didn't like it, and even tried to persuade her with more money than she could count, more jewelry than she could wear, new furniture, and even a car, in hopes of quenching her quest for independence, but again, a determined woman is never easily swayed.

Eventually, she did find a job, one that called for her to work every day during the week and on the other side of town, which infuriated my father. But, he was hopeful she would soon tire of the journey to the other part of the city, come to her senses, and return to her previous occupation of keeping his home, but she didn't. She had been bitten by the bug of desire that urged her to keep on going, keep on pushing, and refuse to go back.

It was during this time that the abuse escalated. Their arguments reached a fever pitch with screams and shouts, chasing me far away from home in order to escape the war zone our home had become.

I occupied my time with after-school sports and activities, rode the subway for hours, and stayed at friends' homes, until it was necessary to enter the place of war to get what was essential to make it a few more days. I never lacked money. After all, my parents' personal war never affected my father's business. If anything, it gave him a welcome outlet, as well as feeding his need to be in control. I imagine in his mind, at least, he was still "The Man" on the streets.

Words turned into cussing matches. My mother had found her voice, realized her self-worth, and accusations about affairs she once overlooked were expressed. Slaps and blows were exchanged. My father even turned the tables on the accusations, pointing in her direction. In his mind, what other reason would she want to venture away from the secure and safe place of his castle? It very well couldn't be attributed to the satisfaction of work or even payment for doing so, it had to be a newfound love, right? Unfortunately, my father never understood that to my mother, his castle was nothing more than a dungeon sucking the very life out of her every day. Though he knew from firsthand experience what it meant to earn respect and have your own job, he could not afford for her to share this sentiment.

As a result of my mother's reincarnation, my father thought his wife was being ungrateful and disrespectful. My mother thought her husband was crazy; she had put up with his antics long enough. Her newfound self provided the confidence she needed to stand her ground and look at him in a totally different light. He was no longer the debonair man who had swept her off her feet on the north side of town. The money he used to flash before her eyes, causing her mouth to drool, was now met with a shake of her head and a suck of her teeth. She even shared her displeasure with me by calling him crazy and wanting to leave. My mother said he threatened the life of anyone who tried to leave. Listening to her, it was as if the blood pumping in her heart was nothing more than liquid fear.

I never heard her speak this way before. I suppose she never had a reason to in the past, but now she was alive within. My mother had been given a glimpse of her possibilities and what life had to offer her with or without him. She removed the blinders he had given her long ago which she willingly accepted—so much so she had forgotten they were there. She was alive and vowed within her heart to never return to that state of unconsciousness again.

I cannot say whether or not I was happy or unhappy with my mother's newfound sense of self. I only wanted the fighting to cease and played my part in the production by remaining in the wings or the backdrop of their lives. Even with what she shared, I had enough sense to harbor it in my heart and never repeat it to anyone—especially my father. However, I never thought things would transpire as they did.

There wasn't anything unusual about that day. My day was spent sitting on the front step, riding my bike, or going back and forth to the corner store, out of boredom more than anything else. In addition, I waited for the night to come, along with hope of a cooler temperature.

Their arrival home was the norm. My mother went about preparing a meal for her family, followed by my father's arrival. By this time, they weren't cordial and rarely acknowledged the other's existence. Words were rarely exchanged; if they were, it might ignite the fuse of the dynamite.

We had long ago dispensed with the tradition of family dinners around a table. Whenever anyone was ready to eat, he or she did. My father went about his daily routine, while my mother busied herself with menial housework. I made my usual exit when they were both within the vicinity of each other. My exits usually led me to the subway where I could ride to any part of the city, far away from home. My bicycle kept me closer or I even used my little car, if business needed to be handled.

On this particular day, my mode of transportation was my bicycle. A girls' ten-speed, which meant it didn't have a crossbar, plus the seat was much more comfortable. It was beige with orange and brown stripes and boasted the manufacturer "Huffy" on the side. I taught myself to ride this bike while extending my arms high above my head for blocks at a time, a feat that took a great deal of practice, but one I had mastered. I darted between cars, past cars, and around cars, thinking the streets rightfully belonged to me and my bike. I loved to ride this bike, but was always careful not to go too far because of traveling the same distance to return, which could be quite tiring.

I don't know how long I was gone, for time didn't mean anything to me then, not on a beautiful day on a bicycle while the winds whipped through your hair. But, I do know that the sun had already set and the street lights were shining bright.

Upon returning to my hood, I talked with my friends for a moment, shared a lighthearted laugh, and even sat down while lightning bugs buzzed around our heads and music drifted from some unknown source, causing us to tap our feet or sway. When I arrived home, I could see the lights from the living room. I carried my bicycle up the steps onto the enclosed porch. I could never leave something as meaningful as a bicycle, much less something as insignificant as a spin top outside, for some passersby might claim it for their own.

I parked my bike in its usual spot and walked into our home where all was quiet. Lights were on, but there was no one to be found. This atmosphere wasn't unusual, and I did not question it; I simply went to my room to watch television. Before turning on the television, I leaned on the ledge in front of my window and peered into the nighttime sky. My bedroom window overlooked our back yard, the alley that was forever littered with broken glass, candy wrappers, animal feces, and beer bottles. I could see the roofs of houses at least two or three streets over. Many nights I heard the conversations of people walking through the alley, drunken tirades of lush heads, footsteps of children, spats between lovers, or even the pants, huffs, and puffs of those same lovers, if they decided to engage in an after-quarrel love session. After taking the visual tour my window offered, I turned on my television, watching from my bed.

Hours must have passed. My television was still on, but the sounds which stirred me from slumber were yelling, screaming, and hands connecting with flesh. Another fight. A horrible fight. Furniture breaking. More yelling and screaming. Footsteps pounding. The sound of shoves, grunts, smacks, and stomps—war. It lasted until I saw the silhouette of my mother coming up the stairs, walking down the hallway, and entering her own bedroom. I didn't move. I couldn't move. I knew that I shouldn't move—perhaps out of fear for what I would see if I had gone to her or fear of becoming the channel to which her retaliation might flow. And so, I stayed in my room. I didn't leave that night; I simply rolled over, closed my eyes, and drifted off, yet again. Until...

He pushed me. I heard my name being called. Was I dreaming? Light streamed into my half-opened eyes, as roaches scattered towards cracks and crevices. He called my name again. My father was calling me, tugging at my arm until I was hanging halfway out of bed. There was urgency in his voice that called for me to immediately chase my sleep away and stand at attention, without fear of the roaches that might dance at my feet.

"She's gone!" he said. As his words hung in the air, he stormed down the hallway turning on every light. He bounded down the steps leading to the first floor, turning on every light downstairs. I could hear him opening and slamming doors and going to the enclosed porch, while his heavy boots echoed throughout our home.

"She's gone!" he repeated and continued his rampage. It still had not dawned on me what he was talking about, but I quickly obeyed his order to get dressed when he returned to my room. "Let's go. I'm gonna find her," he said, his eyes darting wildly, his face contorted in anger.

It was then I realized someone was missing. Someone wasn't there with us. My mother was not here. Is this the "she" he was talking about? If so, where did she go? Suddenly, it was as if his mind took him to another place. He quickly turned around and walked towards me with daggers in his eyes.

"Do you know where she is? You know where she is, don't you? Tell me where she is!" he screamed in my face.

I didn't know, how could I know? I didn't even want to know, but my response was nothing more than a shake of my head, as my body quivered and shook in hopes he would believe me.

He grabbed my arm and half-pulled, half-dragged me down the steps, through the living room, out onto the enclosed porch, and out the front door into the summer night air. I wondered where we were going as I stood in front of our home, before understanding I was to follow my father to the car.

"She's around here somewhere. She couldn't get that far," he surmised as he drove like a mad man, circling our neighborhood, speeding through city blocks, flying across town, and then back to our hood, until the sun threatened to make its appearance.

My mother had left in the middle of the night, and he was on a mission to find her whereabouts. I was curious what finally happened that caused her to leave, but secretly hoped she would not be found on this night, for fear of the consequences, repercussions, and punishment he would dispense.

It was while my father was parking his car, cussing and vowing to find her, that he shared with me his lesson on what he considered the inner emotions of those who are ungrateful and unappreciative for what they've been given. He told me that people like my mother only care about themselves and no one else.

I couldn't truly grasp what he was saying, probably due to lack of sleep and confusion, but curiosity took over my brain, and I asked why she left. He simply told me of his philosophy of the ungrateful, "She ain't care enough to stay."

His words hung in the summer air like a ring of smoke that soon dissipates into a vapor. I inhaled the vapor, and it poisoned my heart and immediately chased away any possibility of sleep. I couldn't speak, but my mind was working in overdrive, as I wrestled with feelings of abandonment and rejection. My mother talked about this crazy husband of hers ever since coming into her newfound self. Yet, she left me with the very man she claimed was crazy. If she thought he was crazy, why would she leave me with him? "She ain't care enough to stay!" If he was such a threat, and she had to leave, then why leave me to be in danger of the same threat? "She ain't care enough to stay!" What about me? I'm her child! Wasn't I worth taking too? Wasn't I good enough to be saved from this man she called crazy? "She ain't care enough to stay!" She was gone, and I was left behind.

In essence, my father, in his manipulative way of turning me against my mother, told me she didn't care enough about me to stay—at least that's what I told myself. I never thought that his words might be meant for him. After all, they fought so much; I thought he'd be glad she was gone. His having control wasn't my issue, it was his. Yet, his wife, my mother, left me in the middle of the night. She left me behind, and she didn't even say goodbye.

I have never known and may never know where my mother went that night. I don't know what neighbor or home became her underground railroad when she decided to take flight. Upon reaching my grandmother's home, she did return days later to take me with her. But, in a matter of days, I was sent back to my father because of his constant threats to harm everyone that stood in the way of keeping me from him; however, the damage had already been done. The seed of abandonment and rejection had already been planted, and those seeds sprouted in my heart.

It wasn't until years later, as an adult, I was able to ask my mother what happened on the night she left. With tears in her eyes, she explained the evil threat against her life that had been spoken and her need to flee or pay the ultimate consequence. She told me she wanted to take me with her, but she was afraid of being caught by her husband. As an adult, I now understand her fear and her need to be freed of him, but it took years for me to come to terms with it, for in securing her freedom, I became a prisoner of abandonment and rejection.

When children suffer abandonment by an adult, they place

the blame on themselves. They feel they were left behind because of some negative quality within themselves that kept them from being worthy enough to be saved. When children are left behind, their minds cannot fathom, understand, or come to the conclusion that the situation is what's best for all involved or is necessary for their well-being. All they know is they were abandoned. If they had been better, worthy of love, or a "good" little girl or boy, then the abandonment would not have happened.

When children suffer rejection by an adult, again, they place the blame on themselves. They wonder what it is about them that caused the adult to move away from them, as if they carry the plague. They believe the distance was brought about because of a flaw they possess. Children feel as if they weren't good enough to be accepted. Children never give any thought to the rejection being the fault of the adult, because children don't know any better. Their minds process information differently than adults. In children's minds, the adult knows better than they do. It's not like they were rejected by another child. In that case, they would possibly blame the rejection on the other child, for they are equals. But, an adult—especially one who should be a protector—knows better, which causes the child to question themselves, their worth, and even the importance of their existence.

Both abandonment and rejection share similar characteristics. They possess the ability to exist even within the physical presence of others, for they are matters of the heart and the mind. An individual can reject someone, yet remain in their presence; the mental and emotional ties have been severed. An individual can abandon someone mentally and emotionally, yet still sit next to them and even hold a conversation with them, although the words exchanged hold no real value.

This is what happened with my parents. My mother had already rejected my father in her mind, wanting to have absolutely nothing to do with him. Yet, they coexisted under the same roof. Her decision to eject herself from his presence and our home sealed the fate of their relationship. In turn, the abandonment and rejection she harbored within her heart, and eventually acted upon, affected me two ways—my mother's departure and my father's manipulation.

In experiencing both abandonment and rejection, I struggled with my self-worth and wondered if I was cared for and loved. I didn't know what was lost or how to regain what was lost. Even my blessed relationships with my husband, a wonderful man of God, and my two beautiful children could not replace my childhood experience of being abandoned and rejected.

Their unconditional love couldn't truly heal my pain. Their smiles, their encouragement, and the joy in having them helped to soothe the pain, but they weren't the antidote. After all, nothing can melt your heart more than finding true love or your child clasping her hands around your neck, planting butterfly kisses on your cheeks. Still, being abandoned and rejected left an indelible wound they could not touch, for it was housed deep within.

This seed which had grown into a plant, this wound that festered inside, molded and shaped my interactions with others. I did venture into relationships. However, fearing the relationship would end and I would be rejected and abandoned again, I became the abandoner and the rejecter, in order to deny myself the pain. If I found myself becoming too close to someone, I shied away and pulled back, telling myself I was justified because in the end, the innocent party would end up leaving anyway. I was afraid to open my heart to anyone. I had many friends and enjoyed my friendships, but was sure to keep an invisible line or wall between us, in order to protect myself from the risk of being abandoned or rejected. I even told myself I was living my life to the fullest. But, deep down inside, there was this little girl who stood in a dark room wondering why she had been left behind.

I blamed myself, and so never looked for the source of answers to my dilemma.

It took the balm of Gilead, supplied by my Father, to heal so deep a pain. In coming to know my Father, I realized that He too had been rejected by those that He loved. The prophet Isaiah tells us in chapter 53, verses 2-4:

> For he shall grow up before him as a tender plant, and as a root out of a dry ground: he hath no form nor comeliness; and when we shall see him, there is no beauty that we should desire him.
> 3He is despised and rejected of men; a man of sorrows, and acquainted with grief: and we hid as it were our faces from him; he was despised, and we esteemed him not.
> 4Surely he hath borne our griefs, and carried our sorrows: yet we did esteem him stricken, smitten of God, and afflicted.

It is also my brother, John, known as the disciple Jesus loved, who confirms the prophet's report in John 1:10-12:

> He was in the world, and the world was made by him, and the world knew him not.
> 11He came unto his own, and his own received him not.
> 12But as many as received him, to them gave he power to become the sons of God, even to them that believe on his name:

My Savior knew what it meant and what it felt like to exist, and all of the emotions that people experience by simply being. He found joy in having little children come unto Him (Matthew 19:14); He shed tears (John 11:35); He knew of anger when He entered the temple and saw the spectacle of the merchants selling their goods in the place that was designated for worship (Mark 11:15). He had compassion for and healed the blind during His earthly ministry (Matthew 20:30-34) and loved us as His Father loved Him (John 15:12). But despite all that He did by ministering to the masses, He was abandoned and rejected—even more so, for those that did so were created by Him, and He ultimately gave His life for them.

Knowing the sacrifice made for me and understanding my Father gave of Himself for me, I learned the true meaning of forgiveness. I had to come to terms with what had happened without understanding the details of the events that transpired between my parents; I had to make a decision. I could be resentful and harbor negative feelings within, denying me the right to truly live and prosper, or I could accept what had happened and move on in my new life in Christ. I had to ask myself if the answers given were enough. If not, I had to decide to take the next step forward, move backward, or remain stagnant.

By understanding the sacrifice made for me, even before I was thought of and conceived by a mother and father who fought a battle not meant for me, I learned of my Father's love that heals what cannot be diagnosed and mends what is broken.

It is His love that reminds me the Creator, my Father, will not reject or abandon what He has created. If there is a parting of the ways, it is solely because of a decision I made to move away from Him, for He promised His children "Never will I leave you; never will I forsake you." (Hebrews 13:5b).

It is by coming to terms with a love only He can give and a promise only He can speak and keep that I find stability and security. He alone walks and talks with me all hours of the day and night. He alone carries me from day to day, even as I slumber and the clock continues to tick. Even during difficult days, when tears are shed, pain is felt, or the sun appears to cease shining in my world, He is there with me.

"In the Garden," a hymn by C. Austin Miles, brings comfort and assures me of His forever presence:

> And He walks with me, and He talks with me,
> And He tells me I am His own;
> And the joy we share as we tarry there,
> None other has ever known.

He confirms that I belong to Him, that I am His child, His daughter; therefore, I am His heir. I am entitled to all He has, all He owns, and all He possesses. If I know this, what do I have to fear? What man, woman, storm, or circumstance is bigger than my Father? What is it that I might encounter that He can't handle?

Even when life is done, my journey has come to an end, and I stand at the brink of the unknown, I can speak as David did, "Yea, though I walk through the valley of the shadow of death, I will fear no evil: for thou art with me; thy rod and thy staff they comfort me." (Psalm 23:4)

It is in His arms that comfort resides when feelings of worthlessness knock on the door of my heart. By abiding and dwelling in Him, I am strengthened, renewed, and never, ever alone.

Today, the anger that used to reside in my heart and the seeds that were planted have been uprooted. He has replaced them with His love, His joy, His peace, and a resolve to walk in His will and His way, forever knowing that He will be with me, "even until the end of the world" (Matthew 28:20).

CONCLUSION

No one can charter the course of their lives. No one has the ability to control every aspect of every moment or even to write their story before it happens. Each day our Father gives is a blessing, and each day is also filled with encounters, experiences, circumstances, and situations that help us become the person He wants. Things never just occur within our lives—everything happens for a reason. However, as humans, all we can control are our responses to the life that confronts us and the actions we choose to take.

Looking into the rearview mirror of life, it would be easy to chalk things up to happenstance or simply ignore them as mere coincidences. I have and always will love my father and mother unconditionally. I realize it was by God's design they were destined to be my parents.

I could investigate my father's upbringing or attempt to perform a psychological screening in order to determine how his mind worked, but what difference would it make? What happened, happened; it is what it is.

I believe my father operated based on experiences he encountered, as we all do, and formed his creeds and philosophies of life as only he could. In his mind, he truly believed that what he taught, his actions, and his lessons were best for him and his family.

As an adult, I cannot hold my father accountable for my actions because when people know better, they are expected to do better. By becoming my own woman, I now know better and am able to acknowledge there is a sovereign God who knows all, controls all, and loves those who are His. People can own, love, and admire themselves when they realize their lives happen to make them better, to mold and shape them into instruments to be used for His glorification. It's an ownership of what I call personal "remarkability," "phenomenalism," and "extraordinarity," based on the Father from whom these things are founded.

Whenever things happen that appear to be less than enjoyable or when our worlds are rocked to the core, it would be easy for us to retreat into safe havens of despair and denial. It might even be convenient for some to point the finger of blame and refuse to see the hand of God working in their lives. We could easily refuse to allow ourselves to heal, but He wants so much more for us. He wants us to take hold of His blessings and enjoy the life He has given us. No longer do we need to constantly harbor hate, reside in resentment, and constantly bandage our scars and wounds, for He has paid the price for us.

> [5]But he was wounded for our transgressions, he was bruised for our iniquities: the chastisement of our peace was upon him; and with his stripes we are healed. (Isaiah 53:5)

We can be healed. He offers healing. He is the healer. Today, this day, is our opportunity to be the people He wants us to be. To stand with pride, confidence, love, joy, peace, a spirit of servitude, and a yearning to glorify the God that we serve. As people of God, all we can ask as we venture through this life is that He will lead us, guide us, direct us, and protect us—and He will. With each step, we must pray, praise and proclaim:

> Lead me, lead me, Savior, lead me lest I stray;
> Gently down the stream of time,
> Lead me, Savior, all the way. ("Lead Me, Savior" by Frank M. Davis)

And He will do this and so much more, for *Father Knows Best*.